with Microsoft®

Windows 10

Windows 10

Shelley Gaskin

PEARSON

Boston   Columbus   Indianapolis   New York   San Francisco
Amsterdam   Cape Town   Dubai   London   Madrid   Milan   Munich   Paris   Montréal   Toronto
Delhi   Mexico City   São Paulo   Sydney   Hong Kong   Seoul   Singapore   Taipei   Tokyo

Vice President, Career Skills: Andrew Gilfillan
Executive Editor: Jenifer Niles
Team Lead, Project Management: Laura Burgess
Project Manager: Jonathan Cheung
Program Manager: Emily Biberger
Development Editor: Ginny Munroe
Editorial Assistant: Michael Campbell
Director of Product Marketing: Maggie Waples
Director of Field Marketing: Leigh Ann Sims
Field Marketing Managers: Molly Schmidt & Joanna Sabella
Marketing Coordinator: Susan Osterlitz
Operations Specialist: Diane Peirano
Senior Art Director: Diane Ernsberger

Interior and Cover Design: Diane Ernsberger
Cover Photo: © photobar/Fotolia
Associate Director of Design: Blair Brown
Senior Product Strategy Manager: Eric Hakanson
Director of Media Development: Blaine Christine
Media Project Manager, Production: John Cassar
Full-Service Project Management: Lumina Datamatics, Inc.
Composition: Lumina Datamatics, Inc.
Printer/Binder: RR Donnelley Menasha
Cover Printer: Lehigh-Phoenix Color
Text Font: Times LT Pro
Efficacy Curriculum Manager: Jessica Sieminski

10 9 8 7 6 5 4 3 2 1

ISBN 10: 0-13-415407-X
ISBN 13: 978-0-13-415407-7

Table of Contents

About the Author

Shelley Gaskin, Series Editor, is a professor in the Business and Computer Technology Division at Pasadena City College in Pasadena, California. She holds a bachelor's degree in Business Administration from Robert Morris College (Pennsylvania), a master's degree in Business from Northern Illinois University, and a doctorate in Adult and Community Education from Ball State University (Indiana). Before joining Pasadena City College, she spent 12 years in the computer industry, where she was a systems analyst, sales representative, and director of Customer Education with Unisys Corporation. She also worked for Ernst & Young on the development of large systems applications for their clients. She has written and developed training materials for custom systems applications in both the public and private sector, and has also written and edited numerous computer application textbooks.

This book is dedicated to my students, who inspire me every day.

GO! with Windows 10 Getting Started

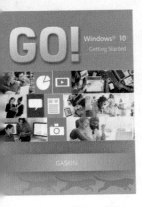

GO! with Windows 10 is the right solution for you and your students in the modern fast-moving, mobile environment. The GO! Series content focuses on the real-world job skills students need to succeed in the workforce. They learn the new exciting Windows 10 features by working step-by-step through practical job-related projects that put the core functionality of Windows 10 in context. And as has always been true of the GO! Series, students learn the important concepts when they need them, and they never get lost in instruction, because the GO! Series uses Microsoft procedural syntax. Students learn how and learn why—at the teachable moment.

Highlights

Easy-to-follow chapter opener includes a detailed introduction to the A & B instructional projects with clearly defined chapter Objectives and Learning Outcomes.

GO! for Job Success Videos relate to the projects in the chapter and cover important career topics such as Dressing for Success, Time Management, and Making Ethical Choices.

GO! Learn It Online Section at the end of the chapter indicates where various student learning activities can be found, including multiple choice and matching activities.

In-Text Boxed Content: Another Way, Notes, More Knowledge, Alerts, and By Touch instructions are included in line with the instruction and not in the margins, so that students are more likely to read this information.

Visual Chapter Summary focuses on the four key concepts to remember from each chapter.

Review and Assessment Guide summarizes the end-of-chapter assessments for a quick overview of the different types and levels of assignments and assessments for each chapter.

Skills and Procedures Summary Chart (online at the Instructor Resource Center) summarizes all of the shortcuts and commands covered in the chapter.

Convenient End-of-Chapter Key Term Glossary with Definitions for each chapter makes reviewing easier.

Teach the Course You Want in Less Time

A Microsoft® Office textbook designed for student success!

- **Project-Based** – Students learn by creating projects that they will use in the real world.

- **Microsoft Procedural Syntax** – Steps are written to put students in the right place at the right time.

- **Teachable Moment** – Expository text is woven into the steps—at the moment students need to know it—not chunked together in a block of text that will go unread.

- **Sequential Pagination** – Students have actual page numbers instead of confusing letters and abbreviations.

Design – Provides a more visually appealing and concise display of important content.

Student Outcomes and Learning Objectives – Objectives are clustered around projects that result in student outcomes.

Simulation Training and Assessment – Give your students the most realistic Windows 10 experience with open, realistic, high-fidelity simulations.

Scenario – Each chapter opens with a job-related scenario that sets the stage for the projects the student will create.

Project Activities – A project summary stated clearly and quickly.

Project Files – Clearly shows students which files are needed for the project and the names they will use to save their documents.

Project Results – Shows students what successful completion looks like.

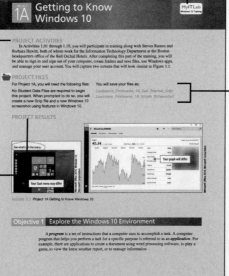

In-text Features

Another Way, Notes, More Knowledge, Alerts, and By Touch Instructions

Microsoft Procedural Syntax – Steps are written to put the student at the right place at the right time.

Color Coding – Each chapter has two instructional projects, which are less overwhelming for students than one large chapter project. The two projects are differentiated by different colored numbering and headings.

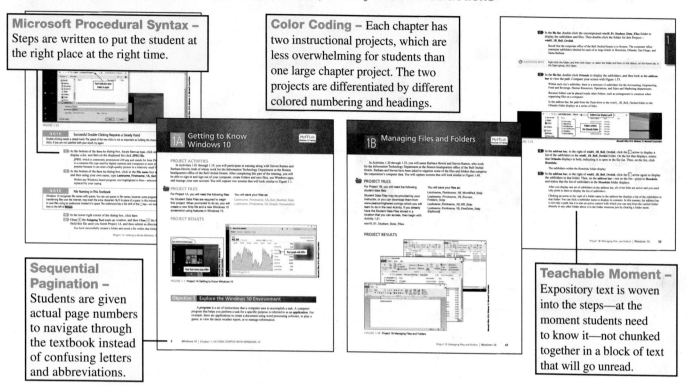

Sequential Pagination – Students are given actual page numbers to navigate through the textbook instead of confusing letters and abbreviations.

Teachable Moment – Expository text is woven into the steps—at the moment students need to know it—not chunked together in a block of text that will go unread.

End-of-Chapter

New Feature

New Feature

New Feature

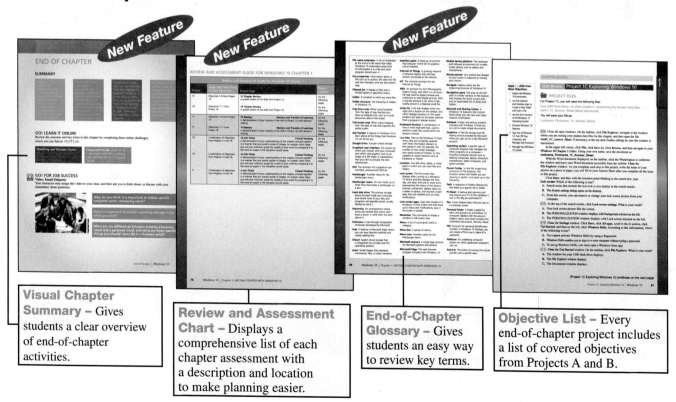

Visual Chapter Summary – Gives students a clear overview of end-of-chapter activities.

Review and Assessment Chart – Displays a comprehensive list of each chapter assessment with a description and location to make planning easier.

End-of-Chapter Glossary – Gives students an easy way to review key terms.

Objective List – Every end-of-chapter project includes a list of covered objectives from Projects A and B.

End-of-Chapter

Content-Based Assessments – Assessments with defined solutions. (continued)

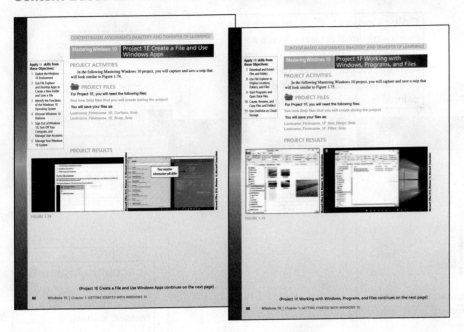

End-of-Chapter

Content-Based Assessments – Assessments with open-ended solutions.

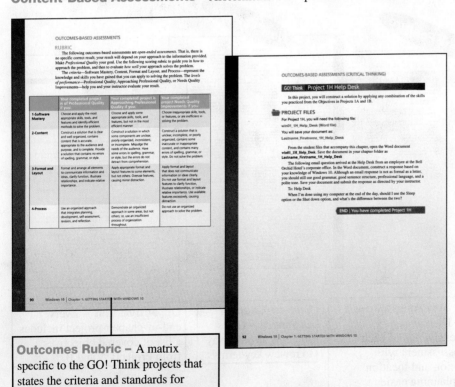

Outcomes Rubric – A matrix specific to the GO! Think projects that states the criteria and standards for grading these open-ended assessments.

Student Materials

Student Data Files – All student data files are available to all on: www.pearsonhighered.com/go.

GO! for Job Success – Videos related to the projects in the chapter cover important career topics such as *Dressing for Success*, *Time Management*, and *Making Ethical Choices*.

Available in MyITLab.

GO! Learn — How videos cover the objectives in Projects A & B. These instructor-led videos walk students through each project.

Instructor Materials

All Instructor and Student materials available at pearsonhighered .com/go

Student Assignment Tracker – Lists all the assignments for the chapter. Just add the course information, due dates, and points. Providing these to students ensures they will know what is due and when.

Scripted Lectures – A script to guide your classroom lecture of each instructional project.

Annotated Solution Files – Coupled with the scorecards, these create a grading and scoring system that makes grading easy and efficient.

PowerPoint Lectures – PowerPoint presentations for each chapter.

Audio PowerPoints – Audio versions of the PowerPoint presentations for each chapter.

Scoring Rubrics – Can be used either by students to check their work or by you as a quick check-off for the items that need to be corrected.

Syllabus Templates – For 8-week, 12-week, and 16-week courses.

Test Bank – Includes a variety of test questions for each chapter.

GO! Series Reviewers

GO! Focus Group Participants

Kenneth Mayer	Heald College
Carolyn Borne	Louisiana State University
Toribio Matamoros	Miami Dade College
Lynn Keane	University of South Carolina
Terri Hayes	Broward College
Michelle Carter	Paradise Valley Community College

GO! Reviewers

Abul Sheikh	Abraham Baldwin Agricultural College
John Percy	Atlantic Cape Community College
Janette Hicks	Binghamton University
Shannon Ogden	Black River Technical College
Karen May	Blinn College
Susan Fry	Boise State University
Chigurupati Rani	Borough of Manhattan Community College / CUNY
Ellen Glazer	Broward College
Kate LeGrand	Broward College
Mike Puopolo	Bunker Hill Community College
Nicole Lytle-Kosola	California State University, San Bernardino
Nisheeth Agrawal	Calhoun Community College
Pedro Diaz-Gomez	Cameron
Linda Friedel	Central Arizona College
Gregg Smith	Central Community College
Norm Cregger	Central Michigan University
Lisa LaCaria	Central Piedmont Community College
Steve Siedschlag	Chaffey College
Terri Helfand	Chaffey College
Susan Mills	Chambersburg
Mandy Reininger	Chemeketa Community College
Connie Crossley	Cincinnati State Technical and Community College
Marjorie Deutsch	City University of New York - Queensborough Community College
Mary Ann Zlotow	College of Dupage
Christine Bohnsak	College of Lake County
Gertrude Brier	College of Staten Island
Sharon Brown	College of The Albemarle
Terry Rigsby	Columbia College
Vicki Brooks	Columbia College
Donald Hames	Delgado Community College
Kristen King	Eastern Kentucky University
Kathie Richer	Edmonds Community College
Gary Smith	Elmhurst College
Wendi Kappersw	Embry-Riddle Aeronautical University
Nancy Woolridge	Fullerton College
Abigail Miller	Gateway Community & Technical College
Deep Ramanayake	Gateway Community & Technical College
Gwen White	Gateway Community & Technical College
Debbie Glinert	Gloria K School
Dana Smith	Golf Academy of America
Mary Locke	Greenville Technical College
Diane Marie Roselli	Harrisburg Area Community College
Linda Arnold	Harrisburg Area Community College - Lebanon
Daniel Schoedel	Harrisburg Area Community College - York Campus
Ken Mayer	Heald College
Xiaodong Qiao	Heald College
Donna Lamprecht	Hopkinsville Community College
Kristen Lancaster	Hopkinsville Community College
Johnny Hurley	Iowa Lakes Community College
Linda Halverson	Iowa Lakes Community College
Sarah Kilgo	Isothermal Community College
Chris DeGeare	Jefferson College
David McNair	Jefferson College
Diane Santurri	Johnson & Wales
Roland Sparks	Johnson & Wales University
Ram Raghuraman	Joliet Junior College
Eduardo Suniga	Lansing Community College
Kenneth A. Hyatt	Lonestar College - Kingwood
Glenn Gray	Lonestar College North Harris
Gene Carbonaro	Long Beach City College
Betty Pearman	Los Medanos College
Diane Kosharek	Madison College
Peter Meggison	Massasoit Community College
George Gabb	Miami Dade College
Lennie Alice Cooper	Miami Dade College
Richard Mabjish	Miami Dade College
Victor Giol	Miami Dade College
John Meir	Midlands Technical College
Greg Pauley	Moberly Area Community College
Catherine Glod	Mohawk Valley Community College
Robert Huyck	Mohawk Valley Community College
Kevin Engellant	Montana Western
Philip Lee	Nashville State Community College
Ruth Neal	Navarro College
Sharron Jordan	Navarro College
Richard Dale	New Mexico State University
Lori Townsend	Niagara County Community College
Judson Curry	North Park University
Mary Zegarski	Northampton Community College
Neal Stenlund	Northern Virginia Community College
Michael Goeken	Northwest Vista College
Mary Beth Tarver	Northwestern State University
Amy Rutledge	Oakland University
Marcia Braddock	Okefenokee Technical College
Richard Stocke	Oklahoma State University - OKC
Jane Stam	Onondaga Community College
Mike Michaelson	Palomar College
Kungwen (Dave) Chu	Purdue University Calumet
Wendy Ford	City University of New York - Queensborough Community College
Lewis Hall	Riverside City College
Karen Acree	San Juan College
Tim Ellis	Schoolcraft College
Dan Combellick	Scottsdale Community College
Pat Serrano	Scottsdale Community College
Rose Hendrickson	Sheridan College
Kit Carson	South Georgia College
Rebecca Futch	South Georgia State College
Brad Hagy	Southern Illinois University Carbondale
Mimi Spain	Southern Maine Community College
David Parker	Southern Oregon University
Madeline Baugher	Southwestern Oklahoma State University
Brian Holbert	St. Johns River State College
Bunny Howard	St. Johns River State College
Stephanie Cook	State College of Florida
Sharon Wavle	Tompkins Cortland Community College
George Fiori	Tri-County Technical College
Steve St. John	Tulsa Community College
Karen Thessing	University of Central Arkansas
Richard McMahon	University of Houston-Downtown
Shohreh Hashemi	University of Houston-Downtown
Donna Petty	Wallace Community College
Julia Bell	Walters State Community College
Ruby Kowaney	West Los Angeles College
Casey Thompson	Wiregrass Georgia Technical College
DeAnnia Clements	Wiregrass Georgia Technical College

Windows 10

Getting Started with Windows 10

1

<table>
<tr><td>PROJECT
1A</td><td>**OUTCOMES**
Sign in and out of Windows 10, identify the features of an operating system, create a folder and save a file, use Windows apps, and customize your Start menu.</td></tr>
</table>

OBJECTIVES

1. Explore the Windows 10 Environment
2. Use File Explorer and Desktop Apps to Create a New Folder and Save a File
3. Identify the Functions of the Windows 10 Operating System
4. Discover Windows 10 Features
5. Sign Out of Windows 10, Turn Off Your Computer, and Manage User Accounts
6. Manage Your Windows 10 System

<table>
<tr><td>PROJECT
1B</td><td>**OUTCOMES**
Start programs, search for and manage files and folders, copy and move files and folders, and use the Recycle Bin.</td></tr>
</table>

OBJECTIVES

7. Download and Extract Files and Folders
8. Use File Explorer to Display Locations, Folders, and Files
9. Start Programs and Open Data Files
10. Create, Rename, and Copy Files and Folders
11. Use OneDrive as Cloud Storage

Eugenio Marongiu/Shutterstock

In This Chapter

In this chapter, you will use Microsoft Windows 10, which is software that manages your computer's hardware, software, communications, and data files. You will use the taskbar and Start menu features to get your work done with ease and use Windows apps to get your latest personal information and to find news and entertainment. You will sign in to your computer, explore the features of Windows 10, create folders and save files, use Windows apps, manage multiple windows, sign out of your computer, and examine user accounts.

The projects in this chapter relate to the **Bell Orchid Hotels**, headquartered in Boston, and which own and operate resorts and business-oriented hotels. Resort properties are located in popular destinations, including Honolulu, Orlando, San Diego, and Santa Barbara. The resorts offer deluxe accommodations and a wide array of dining options. Other Bell Orchid hotels are located in major business centers and offer the latest technology in their meeting facilities. Bell Orchid offers extensive educational opportunities for employees. The company plans to open new properties and update existing properties over the next decade.

PROJECT ACTIVITIES

In Activities 1.01 through 1.19, you will participate in training along with Steven Ramos and Barbara Hewitt, both of whom work for the Information Technology Department at the Boston headquarters office of the Bell Orchid Hotels. After completing this part of the training, you will be able to sign in and sign out of your computer, create folders and save files, use Windows apps, and manage your user account. You will capture two screens that will look similar to Figure 1.1.

PROJECT FILES

For Project 1A, you will need the following files:

No Student Data Files are required to begin this project. When prompted to do so, you will create a new Snip file and a new Windows 10 screenshot using features in Windows 10.

You will save your files as:

Lastname_Firstname_1A_Get_Started_Snip
Lastname_Firstname_1A_Graph_Screenshot

PROJECT RESULTS

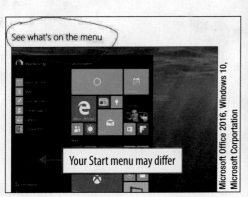

FIGURE 1.1 Project 1A Getting to Know Windows 10

A *program* is a set of instructions that a computer uses to accomplish a task. A computer program that helps you perform a task for a specific purpose is referred to as an *application*. For example, there are applications to create a document using word processing software, to play a game, to view the latest weather report, or to manage information.

An *operating system* is a specific type of computer program that manages the other programs on a computing device such as a desktop computer, a laptop computer, a smartphone, a tablet computer, or a game console. You need an operating system to:

- use application programs
- coordinate the use of your computer hardware such as a keyboard, mouse, touchpad, touchscreen, game controller, or printer
- organize data that you store on your computer and access data that you store on your own computer and in other locations

Windows 10 is an operating system developed by Microsoft Corporation that works with mobile computing devices and also with traditional desktop and laptop PCs.

Activity 1.01 | Identifying Apps and Platforms

The term *desktop app* commonly refers to a computer program that is installed on the hard drive of your personal computer—usually referred to as a PC—and requires a computer operating system like Microsoft Windows or Apple OSX (pronounced O-S-ten) to run. The programs in the full-featured versions of Microsoft Office such as Word and Excel are popular desktop apps. Adobe's Photoshop photo editing software and Adobe's Premiere video editing software are also popular desktop apps. Desktop apps typically have hundreds of features that take time to learn and use efficiently.

The shortened version of the term *application* is *app*, and this is typically a smaller application designed for a single purpose. Apps can run from the device operating system on a PC, a tablet computer, a game console, or a smartphone. You might already be familiar with apps that run on mobile devices like an Apple iPhone, an Apple iPad, an Android phone, an Android tablet, a Windows phone, or a Windows tablet. Examples include games like Monument Valley and Words with Friends; social networking and messaging apps like Instagram, Facebook, and WhatsApp; information apps like The Weather Channel and NFL Mobile; apps provided by your bank to enable you to conduct transactions; and services like Skype or Google Search.

Windows apps are apps that run not only on a Windows phone and a Windows tablet, but also on your Windows desktop PC. Most popular apps have versions for each major *mobile device platform*—the hardware and software environment for smaller-screen devices such as tablets and smartphones. For example, the NFL Mobile app is available for Apple mobile devices, Windows mobile devices, Android devices, and BlackBerry devices.

Increasingly, an operating system environment is referred to simply as a *platform*, which refers to an underlying computer system on which application programs can run. An *application developer*, which is anyone who writes a computer application, must write his or her application for one or more platforms, the most popular of which are the iOS platform, the Android platform, and the Windows platform.

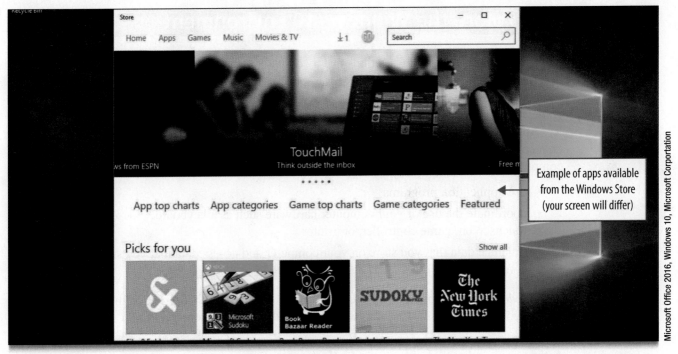

Microsoft Office 2016, Windows 10, Microsoft Corpportation

Example of apps available from the Windows Store (your screen will differ)

FIGURE 1.2

Some Windows apps are also referred to as ***universal apps*** because anyone that wants to develop an app for the Windows 10 platform can use a common code base to deliver the app to any Windows device—a desktop or laptop PC, a Windows phone, a Windows tablet, or an Xbox game console.

App developers can also use this code base to develop apps for Microsoft's new ***HoloLens*** see-through holographic computer and for devices on the ***Internet of Things***, which refers to a growing network of physical objects that will have sensors connected to the Internet. Home automation devices like lights and appliances that you can control over the Internet are among the first objects connected to the ***IoT***—the common acronym for the Internet of Things.

FIGURE 1.3

Bobboz/Shutterstock

1 ▸ A set of instructions that a computer uses to accomplish a task is a _____.

2 ▸ A specific type of computer program that manages the other programs on a computer is an _____ _____.

3 ▸ Computer programs installed on the hard drive of a computer, such as Microsoft Excel and Adobe Photoshop, and that typically have hundreds of features and take time to learn and use efficiently, are referred to as _____ apps.

4 ▸ The hardware and software environment for smaller-screen devices such as laptops, tablets, and smartphones is referred to as a mobile device _____.

5 ▸ The growing network of physical objects that have sensors connected to the Internet is called the _____ _____ _____.

Activity 1.02 | Recognizing User Accounts in Windows 10

On a single computer, Windows 10 can have multiple user accounts. This is useful because you can share a computer with other people in your family or organization and each person can have his or her own information and settings—none of which others can see. Each user on a single computer is referred to as a *user account*.

ALERT! | **Variations in Screen Organization, Colors, and Functionality Are Common in Windows 10**

Individuals and organizations can determine how Windows 10 displays; therefore, the colors and the organization of various elements on the screen can vary. Your college or organization may customize Windows 10 to display a college picture or company logo, or restrict access to certain features. The basic functions and structure of Windows 10 are not changed by such variations. You can be confident that the skills you will practice in this instruction apply to Windows 10 regardless of available functionality or differences between the figures shown and your screen.

NOTE | **Comparing Your Screen with the Figures in This Textbook**

Your screen will more closely match the figures shown in this textbook if you set your screen resolution to 1280 × 768. At other resolutions, your screen will closely resemble, but not match, the figures shown. To view your screen's resolution, on the desktop, right-click in a blank area, click *Display settings*, on the right click *Advanced display settings*, click the *Resolution arrow*, and then click the desired setting.

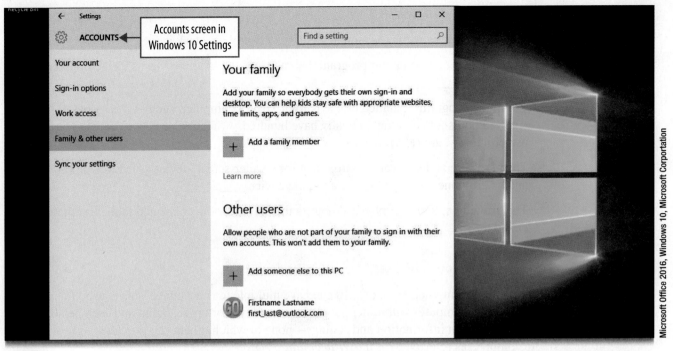

FIGURE 1.4

With Windows 10, you can create a **Microsoft account**, and then use that account to sign in to *any* Windows 10 computer on which you have, or create, a user account. By signing in with a Microsoft account you can:

- download apps from the Windows Store
- get your online content—email, social network updates, updated news—automatically displayed in an app when you sign in

Optionally, you can create a local account for use only on a specific PC. On your own Windows 10 computer, you must establish and then sign in with either a local account or a Microsoft account. Regardless of which one you select, you must provide an email address to associate with the user account name. If you create and then sign in with a local account, you can still connect to the Internet, but you will not have the advantage of having your personal arrangement of apps displayed on your Start menu every time you sign in to that PC. You can use any email address to create a local account—similar to other online services where an email address is your user ID. You can also use any email address to create a Microsoft account.

To enjoy and get the full benefit from Windows 10, Microsoft Office, Skype, and free unlimited OneDrive cloud storage, if you have not already done so, create a Microsoft account by going to www.microsoft.com/en-us/account and click *Create a free Microsoft account*. Here you can create an account using any email address and, if you want to do so, view a short video to learn about Microsoft accounts.

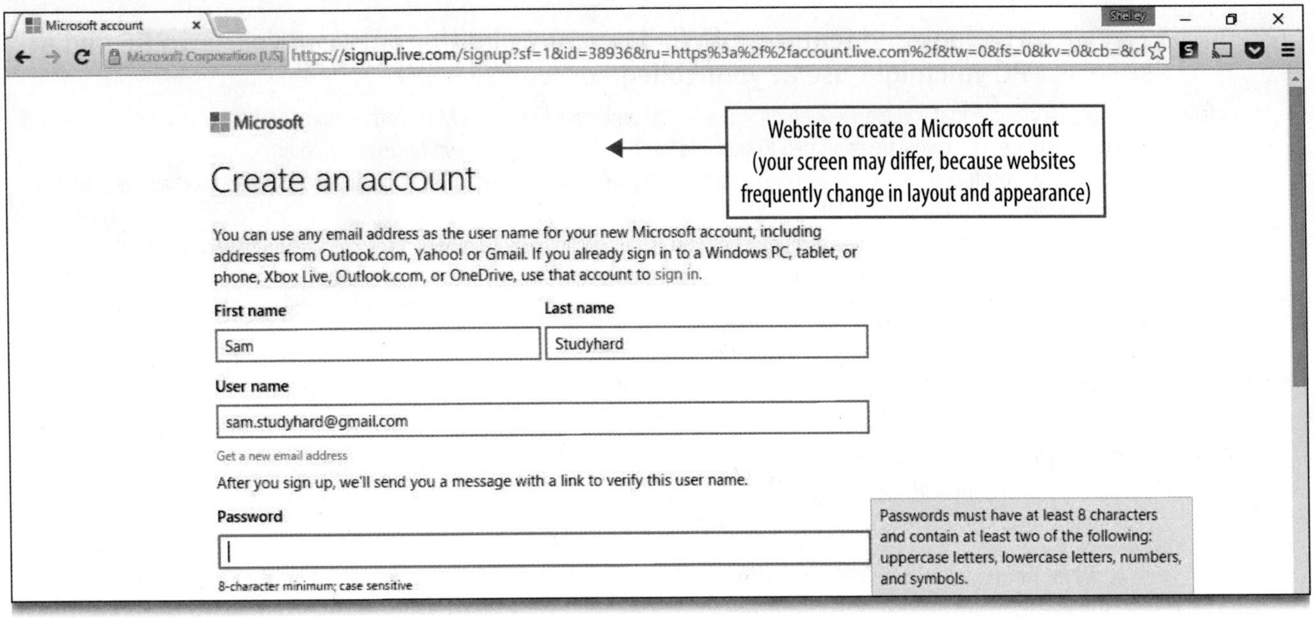
Microsoft account
https://signup.live.com/signup?sf=1&id=38936&ru=https%3a%2f%2faccount.live.com%2f&tw=0&fs=0&kv=0&cb=&cl
Microsoft
Create an account
Website to create a Microsoft account (your screen may differ, because websites frequently change in layout and appearance)
You can use any email address as the user name for your new Microsoft account, including addresses from Outlook.com, Yahoo! or Gmail. If you already sign in to a Windows PC, tablet, or phone, Xbox Live, Outlook.com, or OneDrive, use that account to sign in.
First name
Sam
Last name
Studyhard
User name
sam.studyhard@gmail.com
Get a new email address
After you sign up, we'll send you a message with a link to verify this user name.
Password
8-character minimum; case sensitive
Passwords must have at least 8 characters and contain at least two of the following: uppercase letters, lowercase letters, numbers, and symbols.

Microsoft Office 2016, Windows 10, Microsoft Corporation

FIGURE 1.5

By signing in with a Microsoft account, your computer becomes your connected device where *you*—not your files—are the center of activity. At your college or place of employment, sign-in requirements will vary, because those computers are controlled by the organization's IT (Information Technology) professionals who are responsible for maintaining a secure computing environment for the entire organization.

Self-Check | Answer These Questions to Check Your Understanding

1. On a single Windows 10 computer, multiple people can have a user account with their own information and __________.
2. On your own Windows 10 computer, it is recommended that you create a Microsoft account—if you do not have one—and then use that account to sign in because you will have your personal arrangement of __________ displayed on the Start menu every time you sign in to that PC.
3. To use your own Windows 10 computer, you must establish and then sign in with either a __________ account or a Microsoft account.
4. You can use any __________ address to set up a Microsoft account.
5. Sign-in requirements vary in organizations and colleges, because those computers are __________ by the organization's IT (Information Technology) professionals.

Activity 1.03 | Turning On Your Computer, Signing In, and Exploring the Windows 10 Environment

Before you begin any computer activity, you must, if necessary, turn on your computer. This process is commonly referred to as ***booting the computer***. Because Windows 10 does not require you to completely shut down your computer except to install or repair a hardware device, in most instances moving the mouse or pressing a key will wake your computer in a few seconds. So most of the time you will skip the lengthier boot process.

In this activity, you will turn on your computer and sign in to Windows 10. Within an organization, the sign-in process may differ from that of your own computer.

1 If necessary, turn on your computer, and then compare your screen with Figure 1.6.

The Windows 10 *lock screen* displays a background—this might be a default picture from Microsoft or a picture that you selected if you have personalized your system already. You can also choose to have a slide show of your own photos display on the lock screen.

Your lock screen displays the time, day, and date. From the Personalization screen of Windows 10 Settings, you can choose *lock screen apps* to display, such as your calendar and mail. A lock screen app runs in the background and shows you quick status and notifications, even when your screen is locked. A lock screen app may also display a *badge*, which is an *icon*—small images that can represent commands, files, applications, or other windows—that shows status information such as your Internet connection or battery time remaining or summary information; for example, how many unread emails are in a mail app or the number of new posts in a social media app.

For example, one lock screen app that you can add is Skype so that you can answer a Skype call without having to sign in.

Your organization might have a custom sign-in screen with a logo or sign-in instructions, which will differ from the one shown. If you are using Windows 10 Pro, in the Accounts section of Settings, there is a feature named *Work access*, from which you may be able to connect to your work or school system based on established policies.

Windows 10 lock screen
(your image will vary)

3:20

Thursday, September 3

Microsoft Office 2016, Windows 10, Microsoft Corportation

FIGURE 1.6

> 2 ▸ Determine whether you are working with a mouse and keyboard system or with a touchscreen system. If you are working with a touchscreen, determine whether you will use a stylus pen or the touch of your fingers.
>
> Windows 10 is optimized for touchscreen computers and also works with a mouse and keyboard in the way you are probably most accustomed. If your device has a touchscreen, you can use the following gestures with your fingers in place of mouse and keyboard commands:

NOTE	If You Are Using a Touchscreen
	Tap an item to click it.
	Press and hold for a few seconds to right-click; release when the information or commands display.
	Touch the screen with two or more fingers and then pinch together to zoom in or stretch your fingers apart to zoom out.
	Slide your finger on the screen to scroll—slide left to scroll right and slide right to scroll left.
	Slide to rearrange—similar to dragging with a mouse.
	Swipe to select—slide an item a short distance with a quick movement—to select an item and bring up commands, if any.

3 ▶ Press Enter to display the Windows 10 sign-in screen.

BY TOUCH On the lock screen, swipe upward to display the sign-in screen. Tap your user image if necessary to display the Password box.

4 ▶ If you are the displayed user, type your password (if you have established one) and press Enter. If you are not the displayed user, click your user image if it displays or click the Switch user arrow → and then click your user image. Type your password.

BY TOUCH Tap the Password box to display the onscreen keyboard, type your password using the onscreen keyboard, and then at the right, tap the arrow.

The Windows 10 desktop displays with a default desktop background, a background you have selected, or perhaps a background set by your college or workplace.

5 ▶ In the lower left corner of your screen, move the mouse pointer over—*point to*—Start ▪ and then *click*—press the left button on your mouse pointing device—to display the **Start menu**. Compare your screen with Figure 1.7, and then take a moment to study the table in Figure 1.8.

The *mouse pointer* is any symbol that displays on your screen in response to moving your mouse.

The Windows 10 *Start menu* displays a list of installed programs on the left and a customizable group of square and rectangular boxes—referred to as *tiles*—on the right. You can customize the arrangement of tiles from which you can access apps, websites, programs, folders, and tools for using your computer by simply clicking or tapping them.

Think of the right side of the Start menu as your connected *dashboard*—a one-screen view of links to information and programs that matter to *you*—through which you can connect with the people, activities, places, and apps that you care about.

Some tiles are referred to as *live tiles*, because they are constantly updated with fresh information relevant to you—the number of new email messages you have, new sports scores that you are interested in, or new updates to social networks such as Facebook or Twitter. Live tiles are at the center of your Windows 10 experience.

As you progress in your study of Windows 10, you will learn to customize the Start menu and add, delete, and organize tiles into meaningful groups. Your Start menu will not look like anyone else's; you will customize it to suit your own information needs.

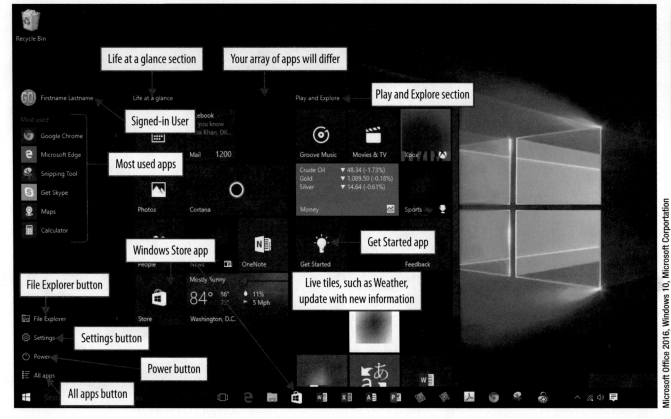

FIGURE 1.7

PARTS OF THE WINDOWS 10 START MENU	
All apps button	Expands the list of apps to show all installed apps in alphabetic sections.
File Explorer button	Opens the File Explorer program.
Get Started app	Displays information to help you learn about Windows 10.
Life at a glance section	Apps pinned to the Start menu that related to your own information; for example, your Mail, your Calendar, and your contacts (People); you can change this heading or delete it.
Most used apps	Displays a list of the apps that you use the most; updates as you use Windows 10.
Play and Explore section	Apps pinned to the Start menu that relate to games or news apps that you have installed; you can change this heading or delete it.
Power button	Enables you to set your computer to Sleep, Shut down, or Restart.
Settings button	Displays the Settings window to change any Windows 10 setting.
Signed-in User	Displays the name of the signed-in user.
Windows Store app	Opens the Windows Store to locate and download more apps.

FIGURE 1.8

6 ▸ Click **Start** 🪟 again to close the Start menu. Compare your screen with Figure 1.9, and then take a moment to study the parts of the Windows desktop as shown in the table in Figure 1.10.

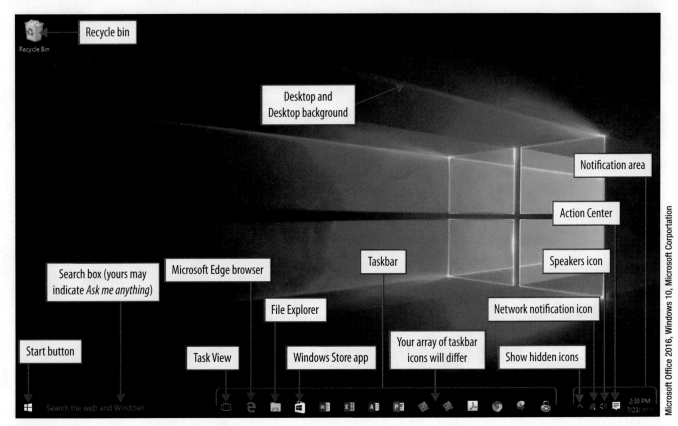

FIGURE 1.9

PARTS OF THE WINDOWS 10 DESKTOP	
Action Center	Displays the Action Center in a vertical pane on the right of your screen where you can see app notifications—such as new mail or new alerts from Microsoft or from social networks like Facebook—at the top and access commonly used settings at the bottom.
Desktop	Serves as a surface for your work, like the top of an actual desk. Here you can arrange icons— small pictures that represent a file, folder, program, or other object.
Desktop background	Displays the colors and graphics of your desktop; you can change the desktop background to look the way you want it, such as using a picture or a solid color. Also referred to as **wallpaper**.
File Explorer	Launches the File Explorer program, which displays the contents of folders and files on your computer and on connected locations, and also enables you to perform tasks related to your files and folders such as copying, moving, and renaming.
Microsoft Edge browser	Launches Microsoft Edge, the web browser program developed by Microsoft that is included with Windows 10.
Network notification icon	Displays the status of your network.
Notification area	Displays notification icons and the system clock and calendar; sometimes referred to as the **system tray**.
Recycle Bin	Contains files and folders that you delete. When you delete a file or folder from a location on your hard disk drive, it is not actually deleted; it stays in the Recycle Bin if you want it back, until you take an action to empty the Recycle Bin.
Search box	Before **Cortana**—Microsoft's intelligent personal assistant—is set up, this will indicate *Search the web and Windows*. After Cortana is set up, this will indicate *Ask me anything*. Regardless, you can type in the box to begin a search of your computer and the web.

FIGURE 1.10 *(continued)*

Show hidden icons	Displays additional icons related to your notifications.
Speakers icon	Displays the status of your computer's speakers (if any).
Start button	Displays the Start menu.
Task View	Displays your desktop background with a small image of all open programs and apps. Click once to open, click again to close.
Taskbar	Contains buttons to launch programs and buttons for all open programs; by default, it is located at the bottom of the desktop, but you can move it. You can customize the number and arrangement of buttons.
Windows Store	Opens the Windows Store where you can select and download Windows apps.

FIGURE 1.10

NOTE   This Activity Is Optional

Complete this Activity if you are able to do so. Some college labs may not enable these features. If you cannot practice in your college lab, practice this on another computer if possible.

Activity 1.04 | Changing Your Desktop Background and Lock Screen Image

As a way to personalize your computer, you can change the desktop background to a personal photo. You can also change your lock screen image to a personal photo.

1 Click **Start** ⊞, just above the Start button click **Settings**, click **Personalization**, and then on the left click **Background**.

2 On the right, under **Choose your picture**, click **Browse**, and then select a personal photo from the **Pictures** folder on your PC—or navigate to some other location where you have stored a personal photo.

3 Click the picture, and then at the bottom of the Open dialog box, click **Choose picture**.

4 On the left, click **Lock screen**, on the right, click the **Background arrow**, and then click **Picture**.

5 Click **Browse**, and then select a personal photo from the **Pictures** folder on your PC—or navigate to some other location where you have stored a personal photo.

6 Click the picture, and then at the bottom of the Open dialog box, click **Choose picture**.

7 Close all open windows.

NOTE   This Activity Is Optional

Complete this Activity if you are able to do so. Some college labs may not enable these features. If you cannot practice in your college lab, practice this on another computer if possible.

Activity 1.05 | Creating a PIN to Use in Place of Passwords

You can create a *PIN*—a personal identification number—to use in place of a password. Having a PIN makes it easier to sign in to Windows, apps, and services because it is short.

1 Click **Start** ⊞, just above the Start button click **Settings**, click **Accounts**, and then on the left click **Sign-in options**.

2 On the right, under **PIN**, click **Add**. If necessary, enter the password for your Microsoft account and click **Sign in**.

3 In the **New PIN** box, type **1234**—or a PIN of your choice so long as you can remember it. In the **Confirm PIN** box, retype your PIN.

4 Click **OK**, and notice that you can use this PIN to sign in to Windows, apps, and services.

5 **Close** ☒ the **Settings** window.

| Objective 2 | Use File Explorer and Desktop Apps to Create a New Folder and Save a File |

Activity 1.06 │ Pinning a Program and Adding a Toolbar to the Taskbar

Snipping Tool is a program within Windows 10 that captures an image of all or part of your computer's screen. A *snip*, as the captured image is called, can be annotated, saved, copied, or shared via email.

1 In the lower left corner of your screen, click in the **Search box**.

Recall that your Search box may be set up for Cortana, in which case it will indicate *Ask me anything*; if Cortana is not set up, the Search box will indicate *Search the web and Windows*. If Cortana asks to be set up, you can indicate that you are not interested or go ahead and set it up.

Search relies on *Bing*, Microsoft's search engine, which enables you to conduct a search on your PC, your apps, and the web.

2 With your insertion point in the search box, type **snipping** Compare your screen with Figure 1.11.

BY TOUCH   On a touchscreen, tap in the Search box to display the onscreen keyboard, and then begin to type *snipping*.

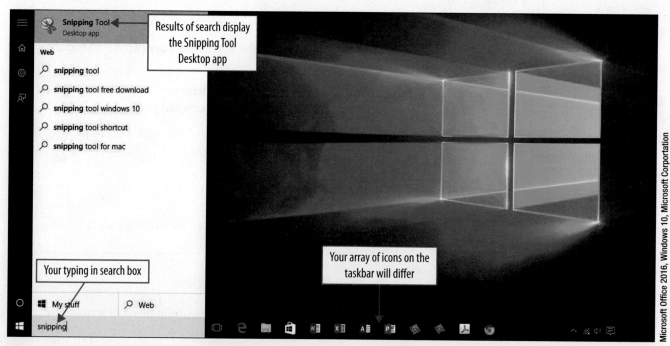

FIGURE 1.11

3 With **Snipping Tool** shaded and displayed at the top of the search results, press Enter one time.

The Snipping Tool *dialog box*—a small window that displays options for completing a task—displays on the desktop, and on the taskbar, the Snipping Tool program button displays underlined and framed in a lighter shade to indicate that the program is open.

BY TOUCH   In the search results, tap the Snipping Tool app.

4 On the taskbar, point to the **Snipping Tool** button 📷 and then *right-click*—click the right mouse button one time. On the displayed **Jump List**, click **Pin this program to taskbar**.

A *Jump List* displays destinations and tasks from a program's taskbar icon when you right-click the icon.

BY TOUCH   On the taskbar, use the *Swipe to select* technique—swipe upward with a short quick movement—to display the Jump List. On the list, tap *Pin this program to taskbar*.

5 Point to the upper right corner of the **Snipping Tool** dialog box, and then click **Close** ☒.

Because you will use Snipping Tool frequently while completing the projects in this instruction, it is recommended that you leave Snipping Tool pinned to your taskbar.

6 Point to an empty area of the taskbar, and then right-click to display a list that contains *Toolbars*—if your taskbar is crowded, you might have to try several times to find an empty area.

7 Point to **Toolbars**, click **Links**, and then on the taskbar, notice the text *Links*.

8 To the right of the text *Links*, click >> and then notice the links to websites you have visited.

It is good to know that these taskbar toolbars are available if you want to use them; however, it is now more common to add tiles to the Start menu for frequently used sites. There are some additional toolbars you might want to explore.

9 To remove the taskbar toolbar, right-click again in a blank area of the taskbar, point to **Toolbars**, and then click **Links** again to remove it from the taskbar.

Activity 1.07 | Creating a New Folder to Store a File

A *file* is a collection of information stored on a computer under a single name. Examples of a file include a Word document, an Excel workbook, a picture, a song, or a program. A *folder* is a container in which you can store files. Windows 10 organizes and keeps track of your electronic files by letting you create and label electronic folders into which you can place your files.

In this activity, you will create a new folder and save it in a location of your choice. You might decide to use a *removable storage device*, such as a USB flash drive, which is commonly used to transfer information from one computer to another. Such devices are also useful when you want to work with your files on different computers. For example, you probably have files that you work with at your college, at home, and possibly at your workplace.

A *drive* is an area of storage that is formatted with a file system compatible with your operating system and is identified by a drive letter. For example, your computer's *hard disk drive*—the primary storage device located inside your computer where some of your files and programs are typically stored—is usually designated as drive *C*. Removable storage devices that you insert into your computer will be designated with a drive letter—the letter designation varies from one computer to another.

As you progress in your study of Windows 10, you will also learn to use *cloud storage*—storage space on an Internet site that can also display as a drive on your computer. When you create a Microsoft account, free cloud storage called *OneDrive* is provided to you. If you are signed in with your Microsoft account, you can access OneDrive from File Explorer.

Increasingly, the use of removable storage devices for file storage is becoming less common, because having your files stored in the cloud where you can retrieve them from any device is more convenient and efficient.

ALERT!

The steps in this Activity use the example of storing on a USB flash drive. If you want to store your file in a different location, such as the Documents folder on your computer's hard drive or a folder on your OneDrive, you can still complete the steps, but your screens will not match exactly those shown.

> **1** Be sure your Windows desktop is still displayed. If you want to do so, insert your USB flash drive. If necessary, close any messages.
>
> Plugging in a device results in a chime sound—if sound is enabled. You might see a message in the taskbar or on the screen that the device software is being installed.

> **2** On the taskbar, click **File Explorer** ▢. If necessary, on the ribbon at the top of the window, on the View tab, in the Layout group, click Tiles. (You might have to expand your ribbon, as described in the table in Figure 1.13; also, you might have to scroll within the Layout group to view *Tiles*.) Compare your screen with Figure 1.12, and then take a moment to study the parts of the File Explorer window as shown in the table in Figure 1.13.

NOTE   Does your ribbon show only the tab names?

By default, the ribbon is minimized and appears as a menu bar, displaying only the ribbon tabs. If only the tabs of your ribbon are displayed, click the Expand the Ribbon arrow ⌄ on the right side to display the full ribbon.

The *File Explorer window* displays with the Quick access area selected by default. A File Explorer window displays the contents of the current location, and contains helpful parts so that you can *navigate*—explore within the file organizing structure of Windows. A *location* is any disk drive, folder, network, or cloud storage area in which you can store files and folders.

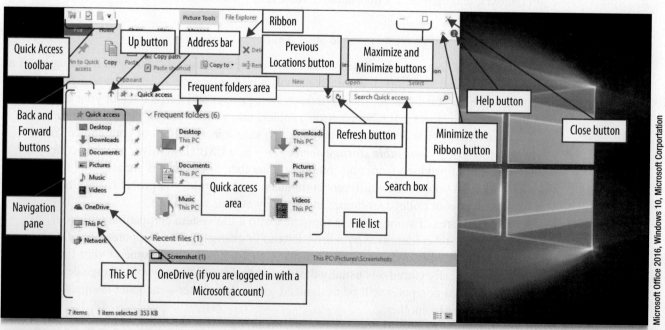

FIGURE 1.12

PARTS OF THE FILE EXPLORER WINDOW	
Address bar	Displays your current location in the folder structure as a series of links separated by arrows.
Back and Forward buttons	Provides the ability to navigate to other folders you have already opened without closing the current folder window. These buttons work with the address bar; that is, after you use the address bar to change folders, you can use the Back button to return to the previous folder.
Close button	Closes the window.
File list	Displays the contents of the current folder or location; if you type text into the Search box, only the folders and files that match your search will display here—including files in subfolders.
Frequent folders area	When Quick access is selected in the navigation pane, displays the folders you use frequently.
Help button	Opens a Bing search for Windows 10 help.
Maximize button	Increases the size of a window to fill the entire screen.
Minimize button	Removes the window from the screen without closing it; minimized windows can be reopened by clicking the associated button in the taskbar.
Minimize the Ribbon button	Collapses the ribbon so that only the tab names display.
Navigation pane	Displays—for the purpose of navigating to locations—the Quick access area, your OneDrive if you have one and are signed in, locations on the PC at which you are working, any connected storage devices, and network locations to which you might be connected.
OneDrive	Provides navigation to your free file storage and file sharing service provided by Microsoft that you get when you sign up for a Microsoft account; this is your personal cloud storage for files.
Previous Locations button	Displays the path to locations you have visited recently so that you can go back to a previously working directory quickly.
Quick access area	Displays commonly accessed locations—such as Documents and Desktop—that you want to access quickly.
Quick Access Toolbar	Displays commonly used commands; you can customize this toolbar by adding and deleting commands and by showing the toolbar below the ribbon instead of above the ribbon.
Refresh button	Refreshes the current path.
Ribbon	Groups common tasks on related tabs at the top of the window; for example, copying and moving, creating new folders, emailing and zipping items, and changing views.
Search box	Locates files stored within the current folder when you type a search term.
This PC	Provides navigation to your internal storage and attached storage devices including optical media such as a DVD drive.
Up button	Opens the location where the folder you are viewing is saved—also referred to as the *parent folder*.

FIGURE 1.13

Microsoft Office 2016, Windows 10, Microsoft Corporation

3 If necessary, in the upper right corner of the **File Explorer** window, click **Expand the Ribbon** ⌄ .

> The *ribbon* is a user interface in Windows 10 that groups commands for performing related tasks on tabs across the upper portion of a window. Commands for common tasks include copying and moving, creating new folders, emailing and zipping items, and changing the view.
>
> Use the *navigation pane*—the area on the left side of the File Explorer window—to get to locations—your OneDrive, folders on your PC, devices and drives connected to your PC, and other PCs on your network.

4 In the **navigation pane**, click **This PC**. On the right, under **Devices and drives**, locate **Windows (C:)**—or **OS (C:)**—point to the device name to display the ⌖ pointer, and then right-click to display a shortcut menu. Compare your screen with Figure 1.14.

> A *shortcut menu* is a context-sensitive menu that displays commands and options relevant to the active object. The Windows logo on the C: drive indicates this is where the Windows 10 operating system is stored.

BY TOUCH   Press and hold briefly to display a shaded square and then release.

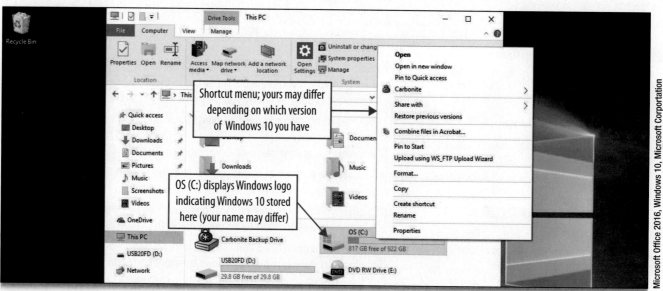

FIGURE 1.14

5 On the shortcut menu, click **Open** to display the *file list* for this drive.

> A file list displays the contents of the current location. If you enter a search term in the search box, your results will also display here. Here, in the C: drive, Windows 10 stores various files related to your operating system.

ANOTHER WAY   Point to the device name and double-click to display the file list for the device.

6 On the ribbon, notice that the **Drive Tools tab** displays above the **Manage tab**.

> This is a *contextual tab*, which is a tab added to the ribbon automatically when a specific object is selected and that contains commands relevant to the selected object.

7 To the left of the **address bar**, click **Up** ↑ to move up one level in the drive hierarchy and close the file list.

> The *address bar* displays your current location in the folder structure as a series of links separated by arrows. Use the address bar to enter or select a location. You can tap or click a part of the path to go to that level, or tap or click at the end of the path to select the path for copying.

8 Under **Devices and drives**, click your **USB flash drive** to select it—or click the folder or location where you want to store your files for this Project—and notice that the drive or folder is highlighted in blue, indicating it is selected. At the top of the window, on the ribbon, click the **Computer tab**, and then in the **Location group**, click **Open**. Compare your screen with Figure 1.15.

> The file list for the selected location displays. There may be no files or only a few files in the location you have selected. You can open a location by using the shortcut menu or by using this ribbon command.

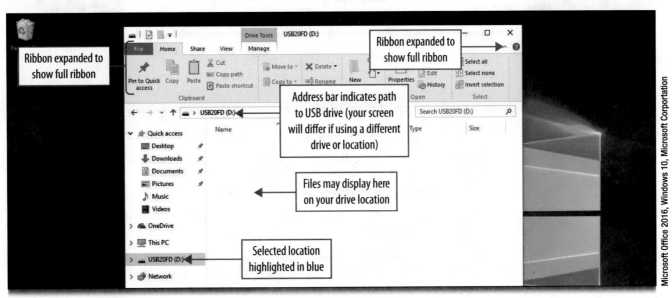

FIGURE 1.15

9 On the ribbon, in the **New group**, click **New folder**.

10 With the text *New folder* highlighted in blue, type **Windows 10 Chapter 1** and press Enter to confirm the folder name and select—highlight in blue—the new folder. With the folder selected, press Enter again to open the File Explorer window for your **Windows 10 Chapter 1** folder. Compare your screen with Figure 1.16.

> A new folder is created in the location you selected. The address bar indicates the *path* from This PC to your folder. A path is a sequence of folders that leads to a specific file or folder.

> To *select* means to specify, by highlighting, a block of data or text on the screen with the intent of performing some action on the selection.

🔁 **BY TOUCH**   You may have to tap the keyboard icon in the lower right corner of the taskbar to display the onscreen keyboard.

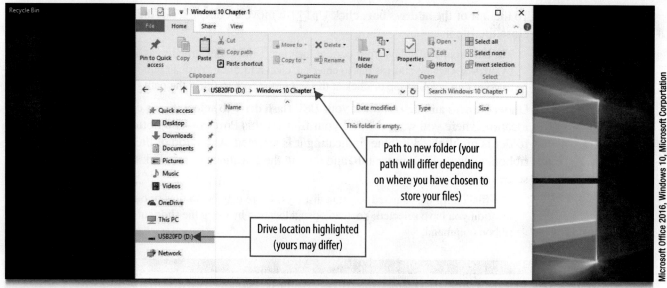

FIGURE 1.16

Activity 1.08 │ Creating and Saving a File

> **1** In the upper right corner of your **Windows 10 Chapter 1** folder window, click **Close** ☒.

> **2** In the lower left corner, click **Start** ⊞, and then at the bottom of the menu, click **All apps**.

The **All apps** command displays the Start menu in an alphabetic arrangement showing every app—both desktop apps and Windows apps—that is installed on your computer. Many apps are installed by default and are part of the Windows 10 operating system.

> **3** Point to the right edge of the **menu list** to display a **scroll bar**, and then drag the **scroll box** down to view apps listed under **G**. Compare your screen with Figure 1.17.

To **drag** is to move something from one location on the screen to another while holding down the left mouse button; the action of dragging includes releasing the mouse button at the desired time or location.

FIGURE 1.17

More Knowledge | **Jump to a Lettered Section of the All Apps List Quickly**

To move quickly to an alphabetic section of the All apps list, click any alphabetic letter on the list to display an onscreen alphabet, and then click the letter of the alphabet to which you want to jump.

4 Click **Get Started**. If necessary, in the upper right, click **Maximize** □ so that the **Get Started** window fills your entire screen. On the list along the left side of the screen, click **Start**, and then click **See what's on the menu**. Then, move your mouse pointer to the right edge of the screen to display the **scroll bar**. Compare your screen with Figure 1.18.

A vertical *scroll bar* displays on the right side of this window. A scroll bar displays when the contents of a window are not completely visible. A scroll bar can be vertical as shown or horizontal and displayed at the bottom of a window.

Within the scroll bar, you can move the *scroll box* to bring the contents of the window into view. The position of the scroll box within the scroll bar indicates your relative position within the window's contents. You can click the *scroll arrow* at either end of the scroll bar to move within the window in small increments.

In any window, the *Maximize* button will maximize the size of the window to fill the entire screen.

It is worth your time to explore this *Get Started* feature in Windows 10 to learn about all the things that Windows 10 can do for you.

FIGURE 1.18

5 On the taskbar, click **Snipping Tool** 🖾 to display the small **Snipping Tool** dialog box over the screen.

6 On the **menu bar** of the **Snipping Tool** dialog box, click the **arrow** to the right of *New*— referred to as the **New arrow**—and then compare your screen with Figure 1.19.

An arrow attached to a button will display a menu when clicked. Such a button is referred to as a *split button*—clicking the main part of the button performs a command and clicking the arrow opens a menu with choices. A *menu* is a list of commands within a category, and a group of menus at the top of a program window is referred to as the *menu bar*.

FIGURE 1.19

7 On the menu, notice that there are four types of snips.

A *free-form snip* enables you to draw an irregular line such as a circle around an area of the screen. A *rectangular snip* enables you to draw a precise box by dragging the mouse pointer around an area of the screen to form a rectangle. A *window snip* captures the entire displayed window. A *full-screen snip* captures the entire screen.

8 On the menu, click **Rectangular Snip**, and move your mouse slightly. Notice that the screen dims and your pointer takes the shape of a plus sign ⊞.

9 Move the mouse pointer to the upper left corner of the white portion of the screen, hold down the left mouse button, and then drag down and to the right until you have captured the white portion of the screen with the Start menu picture as shown in Figure 1.20 and then release the mouse button. If you are not satisfied with your result, close the Snipping Tool window and begin again.

Your snip is copied to the Snipping Tool mark-up window. Here you can annotate—mark or make notes on—save, copy, or share the snip.

As you drag the Snipping Tool pointer, a red frame surrounds your selection; white portion of screen framed

Snipping Tool pointer being dragged to lower corner of screen

See what's on the menu

START

← Get Started

≡

☆ What's new

ℛ Search and help

✎ Setting things up

✐ Get connected

■ Start

○ Cortana

☺ Windows Hello

e Microsoft Edge

◈ Xbox app

⬚ Office

✐ Personalization and settings

☁ Saving and syncing content

⬚ Apps and notifications

⚙ Settings

Search the web and Windows

Microsoft Office 2016, Windows 10, Microsoft Corporation

FIGURE 1.20

10 On the toolbar of the displayed **Snipping Tool** mark-up window, click the **Pen button arrow** ✏, and then click **Red Pen**. Notice that your mouse pointer displays as a red dot.

11 At the top of the snip—remember that you are now looking at a picture of the portion of the screen you captured—point to the words *See what's on the menu* and use the red mouse pointer to draw a circle around the text—the circle need not be precise. If you are not satisfied with your circle, on the toolbar, click the Eraser button ✏, point anywhere on the red circle, click to erase, and then begin again. Compare your screen with Figure 1.21.

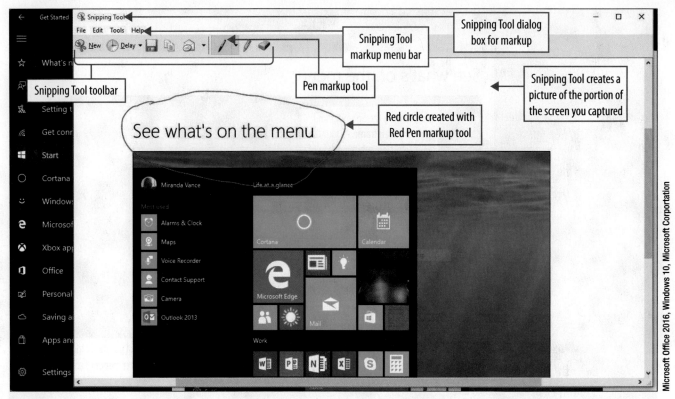

FIGURE 1.21

12 On the toolbar of the **Snipping Tool** mark-up window, click **Highlighter** . Notice that your mouse pointer displays as a small yellow rectangle.

13 Point to the text *See what's on the menu*, hold down the left mouse button, and then drag over the text to highlight it in yellow. If you are not satisfied with your yellow highlight, on the toolbar, click the Eraser button , point anywhere on the yellow highlight, click to erase, and then begin again. Compare your screen with Figure 1.22.

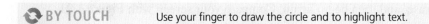

BY TOUCH   Use your finger to draw the circle and to highlight text.

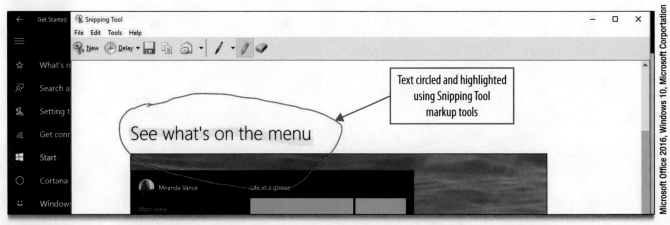

FIGURE 1.22

14 On the **Snipping Tool** mark-up window's toolbar, click **Save Snip** to display the **Save As** dialog box.

15 In the **Save As** dialog box, in the **navigation pane**, drag the scroll box down as necessary to find and then click the location where you created your **Windows 10 Chapter 1** folder.

16 In the **file list**, scroll as necessary, locate and *double-click*—press the left mouse button two times in rapid succession while holding the mouse still—your **Windows 10 Chapter 1** folder. Compare your screen with Figure 1.23.

🔄 **ANOTHER WAY**   Right-click the folder name and click Open.

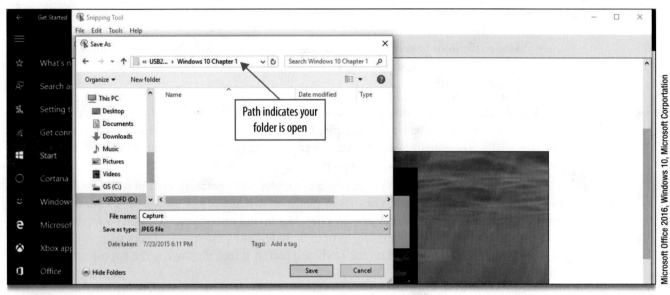

FIGURE 1.23

> **NOTE**   Successful Double-Clicking Requires a Steady Hand
>
> Double-clicking needs a steady hand. The speed of the two clicks is not as important as holding the mouse still between the two clicks. If you are not satisfied with your result, try again.

17 At the bottom of the **Save As** dialog box, locate **Save as type**, click anywhere in the box to display a list, and then on the displayed list click **JPEG file**.

JPEG, which is commonly pronounced *JAY-peg* and stands for Joint Photographic Experts Group, is a common file type used by digital cameras and computers to store digital pictures. JPEG is popular because it can store a high-quality picture in a relatively small file.

18 At the bottom of the **Save As** dialog box, click in the **File name** box to select the text *Capture*, and then using your own name, type **Lastname_Firstname_1A_Get_Started_Snip**

Within any Windows-based program, text highlighted in blue—selected—in this manner will be replaced by your typing.

> **NOTE**   File Naming in This Textbook
>
> Windows 10 recognizes file names with spaces. You can use spaces in file names, however, some programs, especially when transferring files over the Internet, may insert the extra characters *%20* in place of a space. In this instruction you will be instructed to save files using an underscore instead of a space. The underscore key is the shift of the ⊡ key—on most keyboards located two keys to the left of ⌫Backspace.

19 In the lower right corner of the dialog box, click **Save**.

20 **Close** ☒ the **Snipping Tool** mark-up window, and then **Close** ☒ the **Get Started** window. Hold this file until you finish Project 1A, and then submit as directed by your instructor.

You have successfully created a folder and saved a file within that folder.

Traditionally, the three major tasks of an operating system are to:

- Manage your computer's hardware—the printers, scanners, disk drives, monitors, and other hardware attached to it.

- Manage the application software installed on your computer—programs like those in Microsoft Office and other programs you might install to manage your money, edit photos, or play games.

- Manage the *data* generated from your application software. Data refers to the documents, worksheets, pictures, songs, and so on that you create and store during the day-to-day use of your computer.

The Windows 10 operating system continues to perform these three tasks, and additionally is optimized for touchscreens; for example, tablets of all sizes and convertible laptop computers. Windows 10 works equally well with any input device, including a mouse, keyboard, touchscreen, and *pen*—a pen-shaped stylus that you tap on a computer screen.

In most instances, when you purchase a computer, the operating system software is already installed. The operating system consists of many smaller programs, stored as system files, which transfer data to and from the disk and transfer data in and out of your computer's memory. Other functions performed by the operating system include hardware-specific tasks such as checking to see if a key has been pressed on the keyboard and, if it has, displaying the appropriate letter or character on the screen.

When using a Windows 10 computer, you can write and create using traditional desktop apps, and you can also read and socialize and communicate by using the Windows Store apps. With Windows 10, as compared to earlier versions of Windows, your PC has some of the characteristics of a smartphone or tablet—it is connected, it is mobile, and it is centered on people and activities. If, as Microsoft predicts, the laptop and tablet will ultimately merge into one device—like the Microsoft Surface—then you will be well prepared by learning to use Windows 10 and the Windows apps.

Activity 1.09 | Identifying Operating System Functions and Windows App Functions

Windows 10, in the same manner as other operating systems and earlier versions of the Windows operating system, has a desktop that uses a *graphical user interface*—abbreviated as *GUI* and pronounced *GOO-ee*. A graphical user interface uses graphics such as an image of a file folder or wastebasket that you click to activate the item represented. A GUI commonly incorporates the following:

- A *pointer*—any symbol that displays on your screen in response to moving your mouse and with which you can select objects and commands.

- A *pointing device*, such as a mouse or touchpad, to control the pointer.

- *Icons*—small images that represent commands, files, applications, or other windows. You can select an object icon and drag it to move it or double-click a program icon to start a program.

- A *desktop*—a simulation of a real desk that represents your work area; here you can arrange icons such as shortcuts to programs, files, folders, and various types of documents in the same manner you would arrange physical objects on top of a desk.

In Windows 10, you also have a Start menu with tiles on the right. The array of tiles serves as a connected dashboard to all of your important programs, sites, and services. On the Start menu, your view is tailored to your information and activities.

The physical parts of your computer such as the central processing unit (CPU), memory, and any attached devices such as a printer, are collectively known as *resources*. The operating system keeps track of the status of each resource and decides when a resource needs attention and for how long.

There will be times when you want and need to interact with the functions of the operating system; for example, when you want to install a new hardware device like a color printer. Windows 10 provides tools with which you can inform the operating system of new hardware that you attach to your computer.

Software application programs are the programs that enable you to do work on, and be entertained by, your computer—programs such as Word and Excel found in the Microsoft Office suite of products, Adobe Photoshop, and computer games. No application program, whether a larger desktop app or smaller Windows app, can run on its own—it must run under the direction of an operating system.

For the everyday use of your computer, the most important and most often used function of the operating system is managing your files and folders—referred to as *data management*. In the same manner that you strive to keep your paper documents and file folders organized so that you can find information when you need it, your goal when organizing your computer files and folders is to group your files so that you can find information easily. Managing your data files so that you can find your information when you need it is one of the most important computing skills you can learn.

FIGURE 1.24

Managing the data on all of your devices is an important computing skill; storing your data in the cloud—for example, on OneDrive—enables you to access your data from any device

Hywards/Shutterstock

To check how well you can identify operating system functions, take a moment to answer the following questions:

1 ▶ Of the three major functions of the operating system, the first is to manage your computer's _____ such as disk drives, monitors, and printers.

2 ▶ The second major function of the operating system is to manage the application _____ such as Microsoft Office, Adobe PhotoShop, and video games.

3 ▶ The third major function of the operating system is to manage the _____ generated from your applications—the files such as Word documents, Excel workbooks, pictures, and songs that you create and store during the day-to-day use of your computer.

4 ▶ The Start menu's array of tiles is your connected _____ to all of your important programs, sites, and services.

5 ▶ One of the most important computing skills you can learn is how to manage your _____ _____ so that you can find your information quickly.

Objective 4 | Discover Windows 10 Features

According to Microsoft, a billion people in the world use Windows and 93 percent of PCs in the world run some version of Windows. Increasingly people want to use Windows in a format that runs easily on mobile computing devices such as laptops, tablets, convertibles, and smartphones; research shows this is where people now spend more time.

With only desktop apps to choose from, Windows is centered around files—typing and creating things—and that will continue to be an important part of what you do on your computer, especially in the workplace.

Additionally, you are doing different kinds of things on your PC, and you probably expect your PC to be more like a smartphone—connected all the time, mobile, to have long battery life if it's a laptop, and be centered on the people and activities that are important to you. It is for those activities that the Windows apps will become important to you.

Think of Windows 10 as a way to do work on your desktop or laptop computer, and then to read and be entertained on your laptop, tablet, or Xbox game console. Windows 10 is both serious for work and fun for entertainment and social networking.

Activity 1.10 | Using Windows Apps

On your own computer, an array of Windows apps displays on the Start menu immediately after you sign in to a Windows 10 computer. Keep in mind that a workplace computer may have a specific, locked-down arrangement of apps, or no apps at all.

On a new computer, the apps might be preselected by your computer manufacturer and by Microsoft. You can use these right away, and later you can add, delete, and rearrange the apps so that your Start menu tiles become your own personal dashboard. Recall that some apps are represented by live tiles that will update with information after you set them to do so. For example, the Mail app will show updates of incoming mail after you connect it to your email account.

Some of the built-in apps that will come with a new installation of Windows 10 on a consumer PC include:

- Mail, from which you can get email from all of your email accounts, all in one place!

- Weather, from which you can get hourly, daily, and 10-day forecasts.

- Sound Recorder, with which you can easily record a sound, and then trim, save, and replay it on your PC.
- Sports, where you can keep up with all the sports and teams you care about with Live Tile updates.
- News, which is a photo-rich app to keep up with what's happening in the world.

1   With your **desktop** displayed, to the right of Start ⊞, click in the Search box to display the insertion point, type **sports** and then compare your screen with Figure 1.25.

> The *insertion point* is a blinking vertical line that indicates where text will be inserted when you type.
>
> At the top of the results, the Windows Store app *Sports* is highlighted.
>
> Windows 10 comes with some Windows apps already built-in—these include Sports, Weather, News, and Money. These are high-quality apps, and you might want to explore them and pin them to your Start menu. There are other apps in the Windows Store for these same categories, but the Microsoft apps are worth investigating.

NOTE	Don't Have the Sports App?

You can use any app available on your system or from the Windows Store to complete this Activity. The Sports app and the Money app are used here as an example.

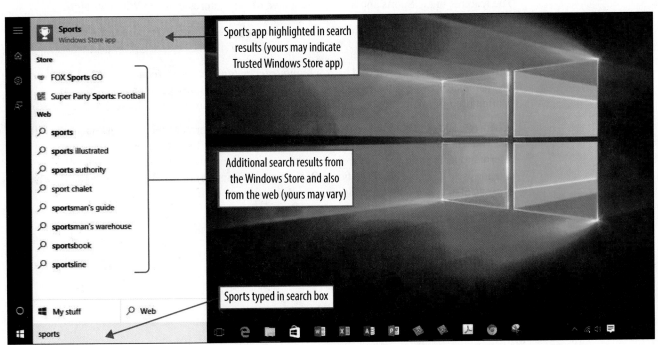

FIGURE 1.25

2   At the top of the list, point to the text *Sports Trusted Windows Store app*, right-click, and then click **Pin to Start**—or if *Unpin from Start* displays, click anywhere on your desktop to close the search results so that the app remains pinned to your Start menu.

3   Click **Start** ⊞ to display the **Start menu**, and then on the right, locate the **Sports** app, as shown in Figure 1.26.

> Up-to-date information may already begin to display.

FIGURE 1.26

Microsoft Office 2016, Windows 10, Microsoft Corportation

4 ▸ Click the **Sports** app tile; if necessary wait a moment if this is the first time you have used this app. In the upper right corner, if necessary, click **Maximize** ☐ to have the app fill the entire window.

Here you can scroll down and click on many new sports stories. Across the top, you can click on *Scoreboard* to see up-to-date scores of games, or click *Slideshows* or *Videos* to see sports news stories portrayed in images or videos.

The features in the Sports app are representative of the features in many Windows apps.

5 ▸ In the upper left corner, click the **Hamburger** icon ▤, and then compare your screen with Figure 1.27.

This icon is commonly referred to as a ***hamburger menu*** or a ***menu icon*** or simply a ***hamburger***. The name derives from the three lines that bring to mind a hamburger on a bun. This type of button is often used in mobile applications because it is compact to use on smaller screens.

When you click the hamburger icon, a menu displays that identifies the list of icons on the left so that you can navigate to more specific areas of the Microsoft Sports app. Sometimes this area is referred to as the ***app bar***. Regardless of the name, you can see that you can navigate directly to categories such as the NBA (National Basketball Association) or MLB (Major League Baseball). You can also create a list of favorite teams that you want to follow.

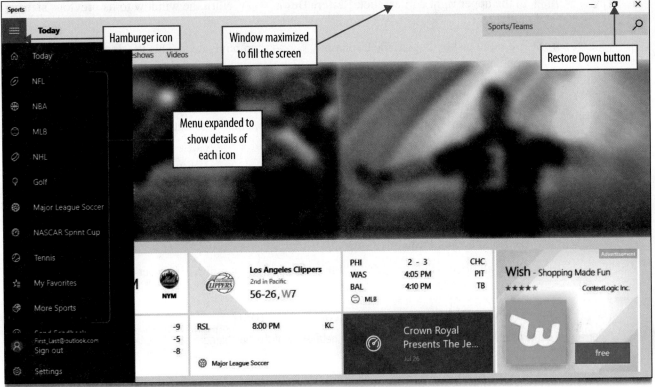

FIGURE 1.27

6 ▶ In the upper right corner, click ***Restore Down*** ⬜ to return the window to its previous size.

Use the Maximize command ⬜ to display a window in a full-screen view; use the ***Restore Down command*** ⬜ to resize a window to its previous size.

7 ▶ **Close** ✕ the Sports app.

8 ▶ With your **desktop** displayed, to the right of Start ⊞, click in the Search box to display the insertion point, type **money** and then at the top of the list of results, click the Window Store app **Money**.

9 ▶ **Maximize** ⬜ the window, and then on the navigation bar at the top of the window, click **Watchlist**. On the list of stocks, click **MSFT**. If *MSFT* does not display, at the upper right, click +, type MSFT, and then on the list that displays, click MSFT to add it to the list.

Information about Microsoft's stock and a graph displays.

10 ▶ Below the graph, click **1 Year** to see a graph representing one year.

11 ▶ With your Microsoft graph displayed, press and hold down ⊞ and then press (PrintScrn); release the two keys. Notice that your screen dims momentarily; you will view the screenshot at the end of this activity.

Use this technique to create a ***screenshot***. The screenshot file is automatically stored in the Pictures folder of your hard drive.

A screenshot captured in this manner from a Windows Store app is saved as a ***.png*** file, which is commonly pronounced PING, and stands for Portable Network Graphic. This is an image file type that can be transferred over the Internet.

A ***keyboard shortcut*** is a combination of two or more keyboard keys and is useful to perform a task that would otherwise require a mouse.

12 ▶ Point to the right edge of the screen to display a scroll bar, and then scroll down to see news stories about Microsoft.

13 In the upper right corner, click **Restore Down** $\boxed{\sigma}$ to return the window to its previous size, and then **Close** $\boxed{\times}$ the Money app.

14 From the taskbar, open **File Explorer** 🗔, and then navigate to **This PC**. In the file list, double-click **Pictures**, and then double-click **Screenshots**. On the ribbon, click the **View tab**, and then in the **Layout group**, if necessary, click **Large icons**.

15 In the **file list**, click one time to select the **Screenshot** file that you captured of the Microsoft graph; if more than one Screenshot file displays, click to select the file that has the highest number.

16 On the ribbon, on the **Home tab**, in the **Organize group**, click **Rename**, and then using your own name, type **Lastname_Firstname_1A_Graph_Screenshot** and then press ⏎.

17 With the renamed screenshot selected, on the **Home tab**, click **Copy**. In the **navigation pane**, navigate to the location of your **Windows 10 Chapter 1 folder**, open the folder, and then on the ribbon, click **Paste**.

18 Close all open windows, and hold this file until you complete Project 1A.

More **Knowledge**	**Where Did the Hamburger Icon Come From?**

For a brief history of the hamburger icon, visit http://blog.placeit.net/history-of-the-hamburger-icon

---

Activity 1.11 | Using Task View, Snap Assist, and Virtual Desktops

Use the ***Task View*** button on the taskbar to see and switch between open apps—including desktop apps. Use ***Snap Assist*** to display a 50/50 split screen view of two apps. Begin by dragging the ***title bar***—the bar across the top of the window that displays the program or app name—to the right or left until it snaps into place. Or, hold down 🪟 and press → or ← to snap the window right or left. As soon as you snap the first window, Task View displays all your other open windows, and you need to click only one to have it snap to the other half of the screen. You can also snap four apps by dragging their title bars into the corners of your screen.

1 Be sure all windows are closed, and then on the taskbar, click **File Explorer** 🗔. Navigate to the location for your **Windows 10 Chapter 1** folder, but do not open the folder. With your File Explorer window open, click **Start** 🪟 and then open one of the displayed apps; for example, Weather. From either the taskbar or the Start menu, open the Windows Store.

Three windows are open with the Windows Store app window on top.

2 On the taskbar, click **Task View** 🗔, point to one of the windows, and then compare your screen with Figure 1.28.

Task View displays a ***thumbnail***—a reduced image of a graphic—of each open window. This command is convenient when you want to see all of your open windows.

When you point to an open window, a Close button displays in the upper right corner so that you can close the window from Task View.

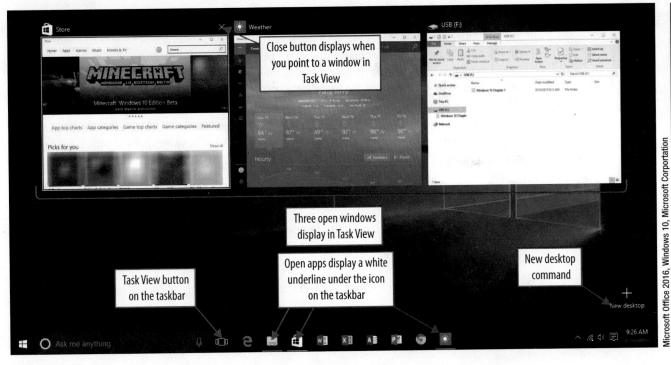

Close button displays when you point to a window in Task View

Three open windows display in Task View

Task View button on the taskbar

Open apps display a white underline under the icon on the taskbar

New desktop command

New desktop

Ask me anything

9:26 AM

Microsoft Office 2016, Windows 10, Microsoft Corporation

FIGURE 1.28

3 Click the **File Explorer** window, hold down ⊞, and then press →.

The File Explorer window snaps to the right side of the screen, and Snap Assist displays the other two open windows on the left.

4 On the left, click the Weather app, and then compare your screen with Figure 1.29.

The Weather window snaps to the left side of the screen.

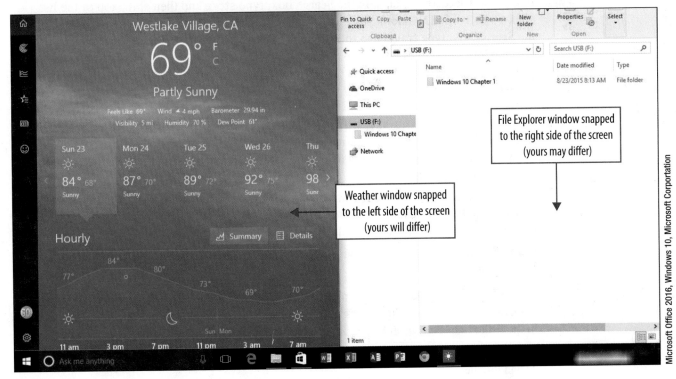

File Explorer window snapped to the right side of the screen (yours may differ)

Weather window snapped to the left side of the screen (yours will differ)

Microsoft Office 2016, Windows 10, Microsoft Corporation

FIGURE 1.29

5 On the taskbar, click **Task View** ⊡ again, in the lower right corner, click **New desktop**, and notice that two thumbnail images display—**Desktop 1** with your two apps snapped and **Desktop 2**.

> If you have a large number of apps open, you can create another *virtual desktop*—an additional desktop to organize and quickly access groups of windows—to work with just the apps you want by clicking + New Desktop in the lower right corner of your screen. This can be a good way to organize and quickly access groups of windows.

> For example, you could run your work email and Office apps on your desktop, and then open another virtual desktop for personal work. Then you can use Task View to switch between open desktops.

6 Click **Desktop 1** to bring that desktop back to full screen, and then on the taskbar, click **Task View** ⊡.

7 From your desktop, drag the Windows Store window down to **Desktop 2**.

8 Click **Desktop 2** and maximize ⬜ the window if necessary, and then click **Task View** ⊡. With **Desktop 2** active—its icon is framed above the taskbar—drag the app on the screen back down to **Desktop 1**.

9 Point to **Desktop 2** and click **Close** ☒, and then in the upper right corner of each open window, click **Close** ☒.

> Create virtual desktops when you need to separate a group of windows while working on other things. Then you can close the virtual desktop when you no longer need it.

Activity 1.12 | Organizing Your Start Menu and Getting Apps from the Windows Store

On your own PC, you will want to organize your Start menu to become your personal dashboard. You will probably use your desktop apps like Microsoft Word and Microsoft Excel for work and school, but with the tiles on the Start menu, you can also use your PC like you use your smartphone—centered on the people and notifications that are important to you.

You can pin apps to the Start menu and then group your apps. You can also name your groups.

1 In the lower left corner, click in the **Search** box, type **store** and then at the top of the list, click **Store Trusted Windows Store app**. In the Store app, in the upper right corner, click in the **Search** box, type **travel** and then click the **Search** button 🔍. If necessary, click in a white area to close the suggested list, and then on the right, click **Show all**.

🔄 **ANOTHER WAY**   On the taskbar, click the Store icon 🏪; or, on the Start menu, click the Windows Store tile.

2 Click to select any free travel app (good ones include *Fodors*, *TripAdvisor*, and *tripwolf*), and then when the app displays, click **Free** (or click Install if your already own the app on another computer) to install the app; wait a few moments for the download and installation to complete ("Open" will display).

3 In the upper left corner of the app window, click the **Back** button ⬅. If necessary, click Show all again, and then find and install another travel app of your choice. When "Open" displays, meaning the app has finished downloading, in the upper left corner, click the Back button.

4 Using the techniques you just practiced, install a third travel app of your choice, and then **Close** ☒ the **Store** window.

5 Click **Start** ⊞ to display the Start menu. In the lower left corner, click **All apps**. In the Recently Added section at the top, right-click each travel app and pin it to the Start menu. Point anywhere in the list to display a scroll bar, and then compare your screen with Figure 1.30.

> The *Recently added* section of the Start menu displays apps that you have recently downloaded and installed.

> The *All apps* command displays all the apps installed on your computer in alphabetical order. You may see recently added apps display at the top.

Recently added section shows the travel apps you just installed

All apps view of Start menu with installed apps in alphabetic order

Your array of apps will differ

FIGURE 1.30

> 6 ▶ Scroll as necessary to locate one of the first travel apps that you installed, and notice that *New* displays under its name. Right-click the name of the app, and notice that from the All apps list, you can Unpin an app from the Start menu, pin it to the taskbar, or uninstall the app. Compare your screen with Figure 1.31.

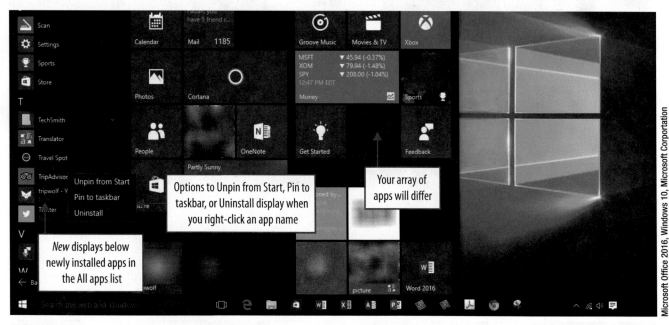

Options to Unpin from Start, Pin to taskbar, or Uninstall display when you right-click an app name

Your array of apps will differ

New displays below newly installed apps in the All apps list

FIGURE 1.31

> 7 ▶ With your Start menu displayed, use the wheel on your mouse or the scroll bar at the right to scroll and locate one of your travel apps you pinned to the Start menu. Drag the app tile into a blank space, and notice that a shaded bar displays indicating that you can create a new section on your Start menu, as shown in Figure 1.32.

> Your array of tiles and amount of space will differ from what is shown, because Windows 10 is *your* personal dashboard!

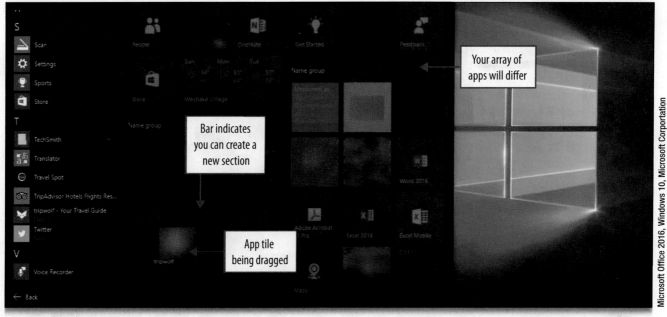

FIGURE 1.32

8 ▶ Drag the two remaining travel apps next to the first one, and then point to the area above the new group to display *Name group*, as shown in Figure 1.33.

FIGURE 1.33

9 ▶ Click the double lines at the right or click the text *New group*, and then type **Travel** to name the group. Press Enter, and then compare your screen with Figure 1.34.

You can use the techniques you just learned with the Windows Store, the All apps menu, and the tiles on the Start menu to customize Windows 10 to be your personal dashboard.

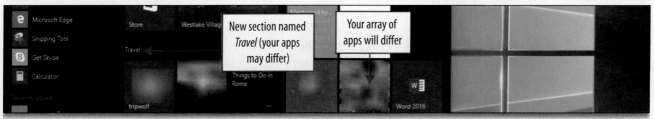

FIGURE 1.34

Microsoft Office 2016, Windows 10, Microsoft Corportation

10 ▸ Point to one of the Travel app tiles, right-click, point to **Resize**, and then click **Small**. Point to another of the Travel app tiles, right-click, point to **Resize**, and then click **Wide**.

> You might want to resize tiles on your Start menu to make them more or less visible—this is another way to personalize Windows 10 to make it work for you.

Activity 1.13 │ Using the Windows 10 Action Center

You probably want your PC to give you notifications—just like your smartphone does—and the Windows 10 Action Center does that. The *Action Center* is a vertical panel that displays on the right side of your screen when you click the icon in the notifications area of the taskbar. The upper portion displays notifications from apps you have installed and from which you have elected to receive notifications. The bottom portion displays Quick Actions—buttons that take you to frequently used system commands.

Both areas of the Action Center are customizable to suit your needs. When you have a new notification, the icon on the taskbar will light up white. There is even a Quiet Hours setting to turn off notifications when you don't want them.

1 ▸ At the right edge of your taskbar, to the left of the date and time, click **Action Center** 🗐 to display the **Action Center** pane on the right side of your screen. Compare your screen with Figure 1.35.

> Although your arrangement and list will differ from what is shown in the Figure, you can see that this is a convenient way to check mail and messages without leaving whatever you are working on.

> You can add sites like Facebook and Twitter to your Action Center.

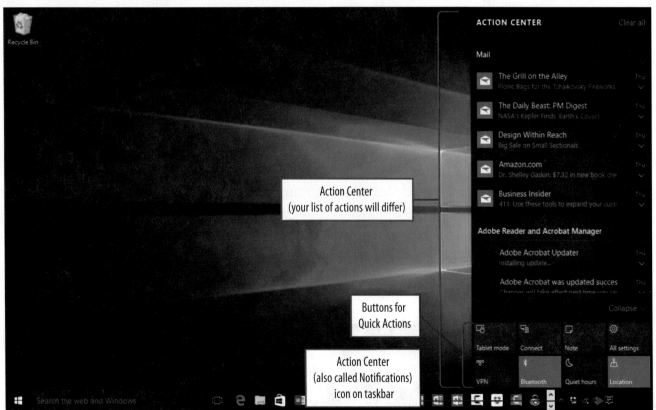

FIGURE 1.35

2 ▸ At the bottom of the **Action Center**, click **All settings**, and then in the **Settings** window, click **System**. On the left, click **Notifications & actions**, scroll down toward the bottom of the list on the right, and then compare your screen with Figure 1.36.

> Here you can make decisions about what apps can send you notifications in the Action Center.

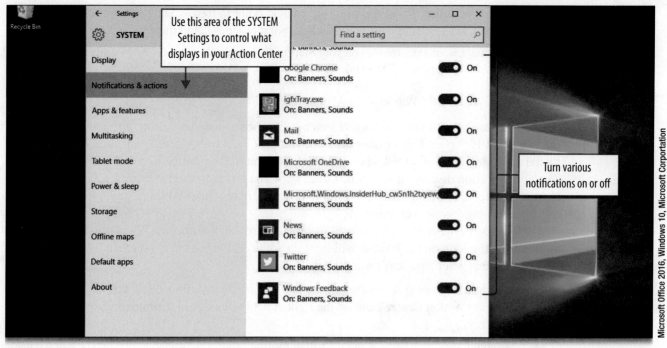

FIGURE 1.36

Microsoft Office 2016, Windows 10, Microsoft Corporation

3 Close ⊠ the **Settings** window.

Activity 1.14 | Using Cortana and Searching for Help

Cortana, the name for the intelligent female character in the *Halo* video game series, is also the name for the personal digital assistant in Windows 10. With use, Cortana becomes more useful to you, and you can add features—such as reminders—that Cortana delivers to you.

On your own PC, when you first use Windows 10 on a new installation or on a new system, Cortana might not be activated. You will benefit from activating and using this powerful feature that can search the web, find things on your PC, and keep track of your calendar.

ALERT!	**Is Cortana Already Installed on Your System?**

If Cortana is already active on your system—*Ask me anything* displays to the right of the Start button—skip to Step 5 of this Activity.

1 In the lower left corner of your desktop, determine whether Cortana is active, as shown in Figure 1.37.

If this area indicates *Search the web and Windows*, then Cortana is not yet active on your system.

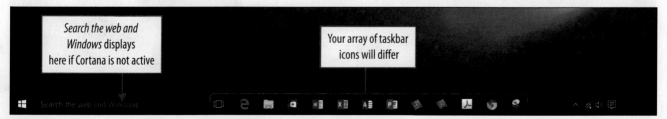

FIGURE 1.37

Microsoft Office 2016, Windows 10, Microsoft Corportation

2 If Cortana is not active, click **Start** ⊞, click **All apps**, scroll down to apps that begin with the letter **C**, and then point to **Cortana** as shown in Figure 1.38.

FIGURE 1.38

> **3** Click **Cortana**, and then in the upper left corner, click the **menu** icon ▤ to display the menu commands. At the bottom of the menu, click **Try Cortana**.

> **4** As necessary, (note that the following sequence of steps may vary, but in general this is what you can expect) click **Next**, click **I agree**, and then type your first name or nickname. Click **Next**, as necessary click **Got it**. Notice that your Search box now indicates *Ask me anything*, as shown in Figure 1.39.

> Usually you will also see a microphone icon so that you can speak your requests to Cortana instead of typing them.

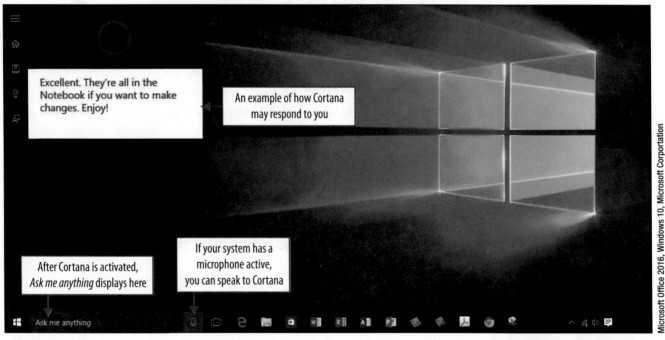

FIGURE 1.39

> **5** Click in the **Ask me anything** box, and then type **who is Cortana?** Then press Enter. If necessary, click *See more results on Bing.com*.

> Your *web browser*—software with which you display webpages and navigate the Internet—displays a Bing search with web links to information about Cortana.

> **6** **Close** ⊠ the browser window.

> **7** Click again in the **Ask me anything** box, and then in the upper left corner, click the **menu** icon ▤. Compare your screen with Figure 1.40.

> On this menu, you can add Reminders to Cortana or add information to Cortana's notebook.

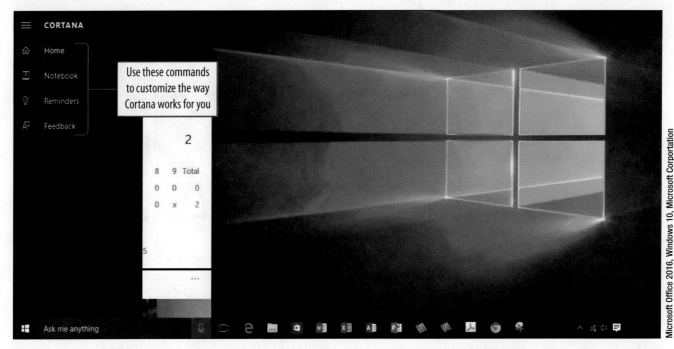

FIGURE 1.40

8 Click in an empty area of the desktop to dismiss Cortana, and then click **Start** ⊞. Locate and click the tile **Get Started**. If you do not see this tile, ask Cortana to find it for you by typing *Get Started*.

9 **Maximize** ☐ the window, and then on the left, click **Cortana**. Click **Make Cortana yours**, and take a moment to read this information.

10 On the left, click **Search and help**, and then click **Search for help**. Compare your screen with Figure 1.41.

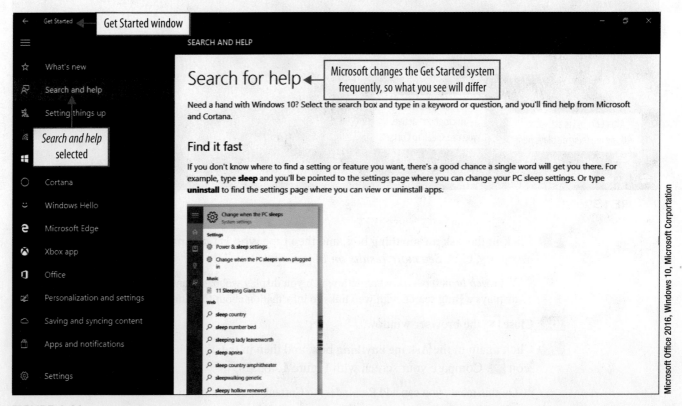

FIGURE 1.41

11 Scroll down and take a moment to read all of the important information.

Because Windows 10 will continue to grow and change and add new security features, rely on Cortana and the web information listed on this page to get help using Windows 10. You will always get the most current information.

12 **Close** ☒ the **Get Started** window and any other open windows.

Activity 1.15 │ Using the Microsoft Edge Browser

Microsoft Edge is the web browser program that comes with Windows 10. Among its many features are the ability to:

- Enter a search directly into the address bar
- Save sites and favorites and reading lists in the ***Hub*** feature
- Take notes and highlight directly on a webpage and then share that page with someone
- Pin a website to your Start menu

1 On the taskbar, click **Microsoft Edge** 🅴. If the icon is not on your taskbar, search for the app in the search box. **Maximize** ☐ the window.

2 In the **Search or enter web address** box, or in the address bar, type the name of your college and then press Enter.

It is not necessary to type a web address; Edge will search for you and present the results.

3 In the search results, locate and click the link for your college's official website. On your college website, search for or navigate to information about the college library.

4 With the webpage for your college library displayed, in the upper right corner, click **Make a Web Note** 🖉, and then compare your screen with Figure 1.42.

The Web Note toolbar displays tools for marking a webpage. Tools include a Pen, a Highlighter, an Eraser, a Note maker, and a Clip for cutting out a portion of a webpage as a file. On the right of the toolbar, there are tools for saving and sharing a webpage on which you have made markups or notes.

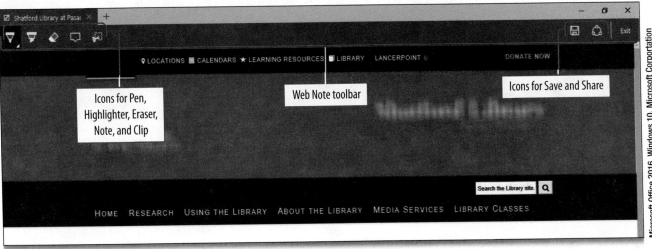

FIGURE 1.42

5 On the toolbar, point to the **Pen** ▽, click the **small white triangle** in the lower right corner, and then on the displayed gallery, click the **yellow square**. Click the **white triangle** again, and then click the largest size.

6 With your mouse pointer, circle the name of—or some other information about—your college library. Compare your screen with Figure 1.43.

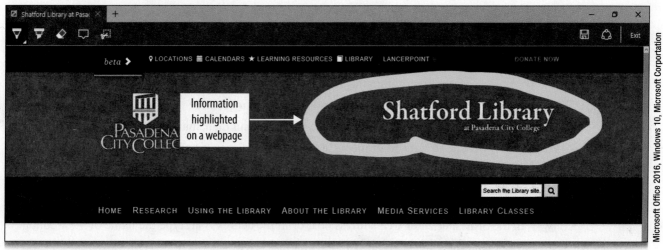

FIGURE 1.43

7 On the toolbar, click **Share** 🔗 to display the **Share** pane on the right, and notice the various ways you can share this marked-up webpage with others.

8 Click in a blank area of the webpage to close the Share pane. On the toolbar, click **Exit**.

9 In the upper right corner, click **More actions** ⋯ and then on the list, click **Pin to Start**. **Close** ⊠ the browser window.

10 Click **Start** ⊞, and then scroll as necessary to locate the pinned website on your Start menu. Compare your screen with Figure 1.44.

Use this technique to pin websites that you visit often to your Start menu.

FIGURE 1.44

On your own computer, when you are done working, sign out from Windows 10, and then set your computer properly so that your data is saved, you save energy, and your computer remains secure.

When you turn off your computer by using the *Sleep* command, Windows 10 automatically saves your work, the screen goes dark, the computer's fan stops, and your computer goes to sleep. You need not close your programs or files because your work is saved. When you wake your computer by pressing a key, moving the mouse, or using whatever method is appropriate for your device, you need only to dismiss the lock screen and then enter your password; your screen will display exactly like it did when you initiated the Sleep command.

When you *shut down* your computer, all open programs and files close, network connections close, and the hard disk stops. No power is used. According to Microsoft, about half of all Windows users like to shut down so that they get a "fresh start" each time they turn on the computer. The other half use sleep.

Activity 1.16 | Locking, Signing Out of, and Shutting Down Your Computer

In an organization, there might be a specific process for signing out from Windows 10 and turning off the computer. The following steps will work on your own PC.

1 Click **Start** ⊞, and then in the upper left corner, click your user name. Compare your screen with Figure 1.45.

> Here you can sign out of or lock your computer, in addition to changing your account settings. If you click Sign out, the lock screen will display, and then on the lock screen, if you press [Enter], all the user accounts on the computer will display and you are able to sign in.
>
> If you click Lock, the lock screen will display.

FIGURE 1.45

Microsoft Office 2016, Windows 10, Microsoft Corportation

2 Click **Lock**, and then with the lock screen displayed, press [Enter]. Sign in to your computer again if necessary.

3 If you want to shut down your computer, click **Start** ⊞, click Power, and then click Shut down.

Windows 10 supports multiple local account users on a single computer, and at least one user is the administrator—the initial administrator that was established when the system was purchased or when Windows 10 was installed.

As the administrator of your own computer, you can restrict access to your computer so that only people you authorize can use your computer or view its files. This access is managed through a local *user account*, which is a collection of information that tells Windows 10 what files and folders the account holder can access, what changes the account holder can make to the computer system, and what the account holder's personal preferences are.

Each person accesses his or her user account with a user name and password, and each user has his or her own desktop, files, and folders. Users with a local account should also establish a Microsoft account so that their Start menu arrangement—personal dashboard of tiles—displays when they sign in.

An *administrator account* allows complete access to the computer. Administrators can make changes that affect other users, change security settings, install software and hardware, access all files on the computer, and make changes to other user accounts.

> **1** Click **Start** ⊞. Above the Start button, click **Settings**, and then click **Accounts**. Compare your screen with Figure 1.46.

Here you can manage your Microsoft account, set various sign-in options, and change your account picture.

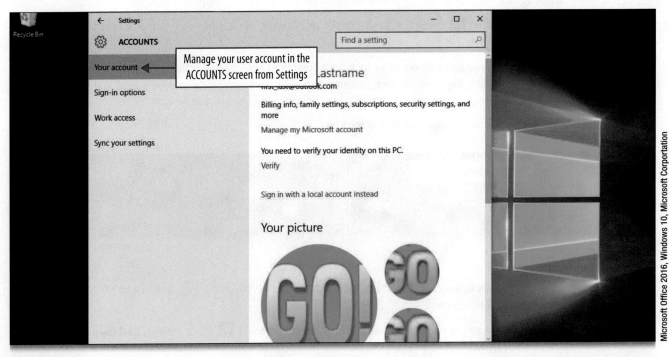

FIGURE 1.46

> **2** **Close** ⊠ the **Settings** window.

> **3** As directed by your instructor, submit the two files you created in this project:
> **Lastname_Firstname_1A_Get_Started_Snip** and
> **Lastname_Firstname_1A_Graph_Screenshot**.

On your own computer, you can change the default settings of some basic functions that will help you manage your Windows 10 system.

> **NOTE** | **This Activity Is Optional**
>
> Complete this Activity if you are able to do so. Some college labs may not enable these features. If you cannot practice in your college lab, practice this on another computer if possible.

Activity 1.18 | Managing Windows Updates, Notifications, and Backup

Windows 10 is a modern operating system, and just like the operating system on your smartphone or tablet, Windows 10 will receive regular updates. These updates will include improvements, new features, and new security updates to address new security issues that emerge. Apps in the Windows Store will also be continuously updated.

Because updates will be automatically installed, you will not have to be concerned about keeping your Windows 10 system up to date; however, you can still view updates and see when they will be installed.

In Windows 10, notifications keep you informed about your apps and messages. You can manage what notifications you get and see in the notifications area of the taskbar from the Settings window.

The backup and recovery tools available in Windows 10 include: *File History*, which can automatically back up your most important files to a separate location; *PC Reset*, which lets you return your PC to the condition it was in the day you bought it; and *system image backup*, which creates a full system image backup from which you can restore your entire PC.

1 ▶ On the taskbar, click **Action Center** ▣, and then at the bottom, in the **Quick Actions** area, click **All settings**. In the **Settings** window, *point to* **System**, and then notice that in this group of settings you can manage your display, your notifications, your apps, and the computer's power. Compare your screen with Figure 1.47.

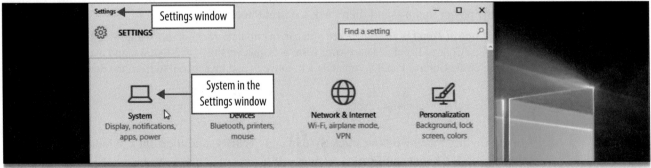

FIGURE 1.47

Microsoft Office 2016, Windows 10, Microsoft Corportation

2 ▶ Click **System**, and then on the left, click **Notifications & actions**. On the right, click **Select which icons appear on the taskbar**.

Here you can select the On and Off buttons to determine which icons display on your taskbar.

3 Without making any changes, click **Back** ← as many times as necessary to redisplay the **Settings** window. Click **Update & security**, and then on the left, click **Backup**. On the right, click **Add a drive**. (This may vary depending on what drives are attached to your system.)

> A list of drives connected to your computer displays, and you can select a drive onto which you could make a backup.

4 Close ⊠ the **Settings** window without making a backup.

More Knowledge | **Consider a Commercial Backup Service Instead**

The backup system in Windows 10 is useful, but you might find it easier to use a commercial backup system like Carbonite or Mozy. For a small annual fee, these systems back up your files automatically on their servers—in the cloud—and if your computer suffers a misfortune, you can get your files back easily by simply downloading them to your new or repaired system.

N O T E | **This Activity Is Optional**

Complete this Activity if you are able to do so. Some college labs may not enable these features. If you cannot practice in your college lab, practice this on another computer if possible.

Activity 1.19 | Managing Windows Defender and Windows Firewall

Windows Defender is protection built into Windows 10 that helps prevent viruses, spyware, and malicious or unwanted software from being installed on your PC without your knowledge. You can rely on Windows Defender without assistance from other software products that might come preinstalled on a PC you purchase; you can confidently uninstall and not pay for these products.

Windows Firewall is protection built into Windows 10 that can prevent hackers or malicious software from gaining access to your computer through a network or the Internet.

1 In the lower left corner of your screen, click in the search box, type **windows defender** and then press Enter to display the **Windows Defender** dialog box.

> Here you can change settings related to real-time and cloud-based protection.

2 Close ⊠ the **Windows Defender** window.

3 In the lower left corner, point to **Start** ⊞, right-click to display a menu—sometimes referred to as the power menu—and then click **Control Panel**.

> The *Control Panel* is an area where you can manipulate some of the Windows 10 basic system settings. Control Panel is a carryover from previous versions of Windows, and over time, more and more of the Control Panel commands will move to and be accessible from the Settings window.

🔄 **ANOTHER WAY** | Type *control panel* in the search box.

---

4 In the **Control Panel** window, click **System and Security**, and then click **Windows Firewall**. On the left, click **Change notification settings**—if necessary, enter your password; or, if you are unable to enter a password, just read the remaining steps in this activity.

5 In the **Customize Settings** window, notice that you can receive notifications when Windows Firewall blocks a new app.

6 Close ⊠ the window.

7 If you have not already done so, as directed by your instructor, submit the two files you created in this project: **Lastname_Firstname_1A_Get_Started_Snip** and **Lastname_Firstname_1A_Graph_Screenshot**.

END | You have completed Project 1A

Managing Files and Folders

In Activities 1.20 through 1.32, you will assist Barbara Hewitt and Steven Ramos, who work for the Information Technology Department at the Boston headquarters office of the Bell Orchid Hotels. Barbara and Steven have been asked to organize some of the files and folders that comprise the corporation's computer data. You will capture screens that will look similar to Figure 1.48.

PROJECT FILES

For Project 1B, you will need the following student data files:

Student Data Files may be provided by your instructor, or you can download them from www.pearsonhighered.com/go which you will learn to do in the next Activity. If you already have the Student Data Files stored in a location that you can access, then begin with Activity 1.21.

win10_01_Student_Data_Files

You will save your files as:

Lastname_Firstname_1B_WordPad_Snip

Lastname_Firstname_1B_Europe_ Folders_Snip

Lastname_Firstname_1B_HR_Snip

Lastname_Firstname_1B_OneDrive_Snip (Optional)

PROJECT RESULTS

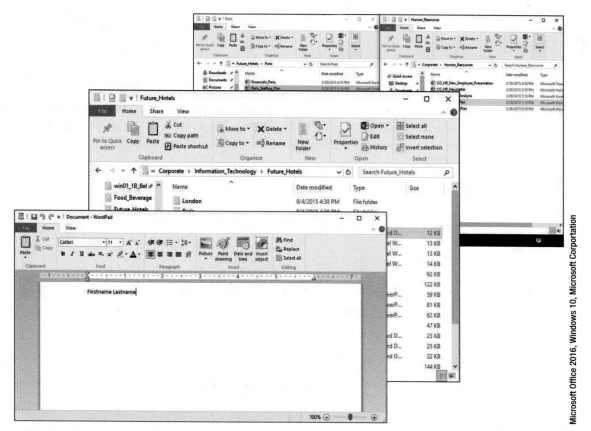

FIGURE 1.48 Project 1B Managing Files and Folders

Microsoft Office 2016, Windows 10, Microsoft Corporation

Download refers to the action of transferring or copying a file from another location—such as a cloud storage location or from an Internet site—to your computer. Files that you download are frequently *compressed files*, which are files that have been reduced in size, take up less storage space, and can be transferred to other computers faster than uncompressed files.

A compressed folder might contain a group of files that were combined into one compressed folder, which makes it easier to share a group of files. To *extract* means to decompress, or pull out, files from a compressed form. The terms *zip* and *unzip* refer to the process of compressing (zipping) and extracting (unzipping). File Explorer includes *Compressed Folder Tools*, available on the ribbon, to assist you in extracting compressed files.

Activity 1.20 | Downloading Files from a Website

To complete this Project and the Projects at the end of this chapter, you will need the Student Data Files that accompany this chapter. Follow the steps in this Activity to download the Student Data Files from the publisher's website; or, your instructor might provide the Student Data Files to you, for example, in your learning management system.

1 If necessary, sign in to your computer and display the Windows 10 desktop.

2 Determine the location where you want to store your downloaded Student Data Files; this example will assume you are using a USB flash drive. If you are working on your own computer, consider the Documents folder on This PC or your OneDrive cloud storage.

3 On the taskbar, click **Microsoft Edge** , click in the **Search or enter web address** box or in the address bar—type **www.pearsonhighered.com/go** and then press Enter.

Microsoft Edge is Microsoft's Windows 10 *web browser*—software with which you display webpages and navigate the Internet.

ANOTHER WAY You can use other browsers, such as Chrome or Firefox, to go to this website. Use the download techniques associated with that browser to download the files.

4 At the Pearson site, on the right, locate and then click the cover image for the book you are using. In the window that opens, under **Student Resources**, click **Organized by chapter**.

5 Click the link for **win10_01_Student_Data_Files**. At the bottom of the screen, when the file has finished downloading, click **Open** to display the **File Explorer** window for the downloaded files, and then notice the path in the address bar.

Typically, files that you download from an Internet site are stored in the *Downloads folder* on your PC.

6 In the **file list**, click the **win10_01_Student_Data_Files** folder one time to select it, and then on the right edge of the ribbon, with the **Compressed Folder Tools** active, click **Extract all**. In the displayed dialog box, click **Browse**.

7 In the **Select a destination** window, in the **navigation pane**, if necessary expand **This PC**, and then click your **USB flash drive** one time to select it—or click your desired storage location. In the lower right corner, click **Select Folder**. In the lower right corner of the displayed window, click **Extract**.

After a few moments, the folder is extracted and placed in the location you selected.

8 **Close** ☒ all open windows to redisplay your desktop.

Objective 8 | Use File Explorer to Display Locations, Folders, and Files

A file is the fundamental unit of storage that enables Windows 10 to distinguish one set of information from another. A folder is the basic organizing tool for files. In a folder, you can store files that are related to one another. You can also place a folder inside another folder, which is then referred to as a *subfolder*.

Windows 10 arranges folders in a structure that resembles a *hierarchy*—an arrangement where items are ranked and where each level is lower in rank than the item above it. The hierarchy of folders is referred to as the *folder structure*. A sequence of folders in the folder structure that leads to a specific file or folder is a *path*.

Activity 1.21 | Navigating with File Explorer

Recall that File Explorer is the program that displays the contents of locations, folders, and files on your computer and also in your OneDrive and other cloud storage locations. File Explorer also enables you to perform tasks related to your files and folders such as copying, moving, and renaming. When you open a folder or location, a window displays to show its contents. The design of the window helps you navigate—explore within the file structure for the purpose of finding files and folders—so that you can save and find your files and folders efficiently.

In this Activity, you will open a folder and examine the parts of its window.

1 Close any open windows. With your desktop displayed, on the taskbar, *point to* but do not click **File Explorer** 📁, and notice the ScreenTip *File Explorer*.

A *ScreenTip* displays useful information when you perform various mouse actions, such as pointing to screen elements.

2 Click **File Explorer** 📁 to display the **File Explorer** window.

File Explorer is at work anytime you are viewing the contents of a location or the contents of a folder stored in a specific location. By default, the File Explorer button on the taskbar opens with the *Quick access* location—a list of files you have been working on and folders you use often—selected in the navigation pane and in the address bar.

The default list will likely display the Desktop, Downloads, Documents, Pictures, Music, Videos, and OneDrive folders, and then folders you worked on recently or work on frequently will be added automatically, although you can change this behavior.

The benefit of the Quick access list is that you can customize a list of folders that you go to often. To add a folder to the list quickly, you can right-click a folder in the file list and click Pin to Quick Access.

For example, if you are working on a project, you can pin it—or simply drag it—to the Quick access list. When you are done with the project and not using the folder so often, you can remove it from the list. Removing it from the list does not delete the folder, it simply removes it from the Quick access list.

| NOTE | You Can Change the Behavior of the Quick Access List in File Explorer |

If you prefer to have File Explorer default to the This PC view—which was the default in Windows 8—on the View tab, click Options to display the Folder Options dialog box. On the General tab, click the Open File Explorer to arrow, and then click This PC. If you want to prevent recently and frequently used items from displaying on the Quick access list, on the same tab, at the bottom under Privacy, clear the check boxes and then clear the File Explorer history.

3 On the left, in the **navigation pane**, scroll down if necessary, and then click **This PC** to display folders, devices, and drives in the **file list** on the right. Compare your screen with Figure 1.49.

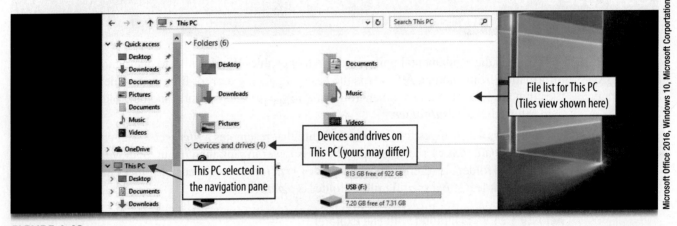

FIGURE 1.49

4 If necessary, in the upper right corner, click Expand the Ribbon ⌄. In the **File List,** under **Folders,** click **Documents** one time to select it, and then on the ribbon, on the **Computer tab,** in the **Location group,** click **Open.** On the ribbon, click the **View tab,** and then in the **Layout group,** if necessary, click **Details.**

The window for the Documents folder displays. You may or may not have files and folders already stored here.

ANOTHER WAY   Point to Documents, right-click to display a shortcut menu, and then click Open; or, point to Documents and double-click.

5 Compare your screen with Figure 1.50, and then take a moment to study the parts of the window as described in the table in Figure 1.51.

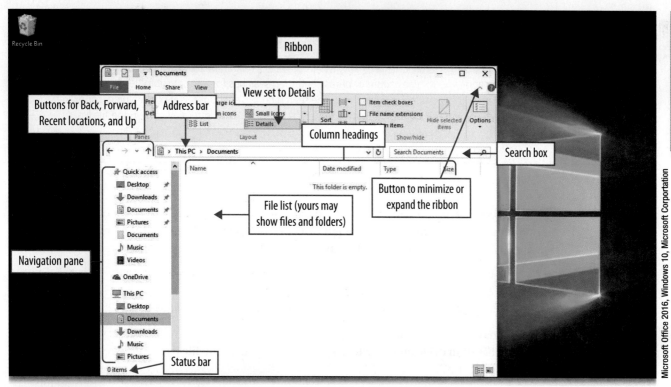

FIGURE 1.50

PARTS OF THE FILE EXPLORER WINDOW	
WINDOW PART	**FUNCTION**
Address bar	Displays your current location in the file structure as a series of links separated by arrows. Tap or click a part of the path to go to that level or tap or click at the end to select the path for copying.
Back, Forward, Recent locations, and Up buttons	Enable you to navigate to other folders you have already opened without closing the current window. These buttons work with the address bar; that is, after you use the address bar to change folders, you can use the Back button to return to the previous folder. Use the Up button to open the location where the folder you are viewing is saved—also referred to as the *parent folder*.
Column headings	Identify the columns in Details view. By clicking the column heading name, you can change how the files in the file list are organized; by clicking the arrow on the right, you can select various sort arrangements in the file list. By right-clicking a column heading, you can select other columns to add to the file list.
File list	Displays the contents of the current folder or location. If you type text into the Search box, a search is conducted on the folder or location only, and only the folders and files that match your search will display here—including files in subfolders.
Minimize the Ribbon or Expand the Ribbon button	Changes the display of the ribbon. When minimized, the ribbon shows only the tab names and not the full ribbon.
Navigation pane	Displays locations to which you can navigate; for example, your OneDrive, folders on This PC, devices and drives connected to your PC, folders listed under Quick access, and possibly other PCs on your network. Use Quick access to open your most commonly used folders and searches. If you have a folder that you use frequently, you can drag it to the Quick access area so that it is always available.
Ribbon	Groups common tasks such as copying and moving, creating new folders, emailing and zipping items, and changing views of the items in the file list.

FIGURE 1.51 *(continued)*

PARTS OF THE FILE EXPLORER WINDOW (*continued*)	
WINDOW PART	**FUNCTION**
Search box	Enables you to type a word or phrase and then searches for a file or subfolder stored in the current folder that contains matching text. The search begins as soon as you begin typing; for example, if you type *G*, all the file and folder names that start with the letter *G* display in the file list.
Status bar	Displays the total number of items in a location, or the number of selected items and their total size.

FIGURE 1.51

6 ▶ Move your ⬚ pointer anywhere into the **navigation pane**, and notice that a downward pointing arrow ✓ displays to the left of *Quick access* to indicate that this item is expanded, and a right-pointing arrow ❯ displays to the left of items that are collapsed.

You can click these arrows to collapse and expand areas in the navigation pane.

Activity 1.22 │ Using File Explorer to Display Locations, Folders, and Files

1 ▶ In the **navigation pane**, if necessary expand **This PC**, scroll down if necessary, and then click your **USB flash drive** one time to display its contents in the **file list**. Compare your screen with Figure 1.52.

In the navigation pane, *This PC* displays all of the drive letter locations attached to your computer, including the internal hard drives, CD or DVD drives, and any connected devices such as a USB flash drive.

Your extracted student data files display if this is your storage location.

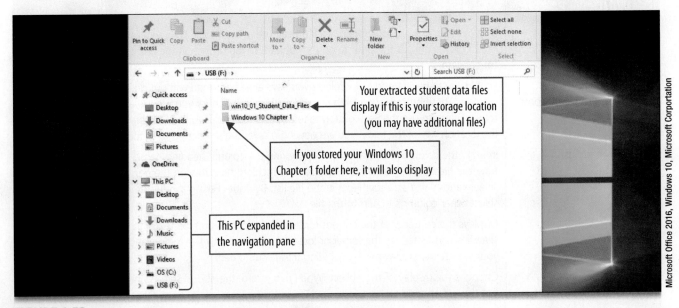

FIGURE 1.52

2 In the **file list**, double-click the uncompressed **win10_01_Student_Data_Files** folder to display the subfolders and files. Then double-click the folder for this Project— **win01_1B_Bell_Orchid**.

Recall that the corporate office of the Bell Orchid Hotels is in Boston. The corporate office maintains subfolders labeled for each of its large hotels in Honolulu, Orlando, San Diego, and Santa Barbara.

⟳ ANOTHER WAY   Right-click the folder, and then click Open; or, select the folder and then on the ribbon, on the Home tab, in the Open group, click Open.

3 In the **file list**, double-click **Orlando** to display the subfolders, and then look at the **address bar** to view the path. Compare your screen with Figure 1.53.

Within each city's subfolder, there is a structure of subfolders for the Accounting, Engineering, Food and Beverage, Human Resources, Operations, and Sales and Marketing departments.

Because folders can be placed inside other folders, such an arrangement is common when organizing files on a computer.

In the address bar, the path from the flash drive to the win01_1B_Bell_Orchid folder to the Orlando folder displays as a series of links.

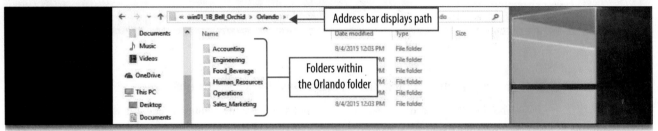

FIGURE 1.53   Microsoft Office 2016, Windows 10, Microsoft Corportation

4 In the **address bar**, to the right of **win01_1B_Bell_Orchid**, click the ⟩ arrow to display a list of the subfolders in the **win01_1B_Bell_Orchid** folder. On the list that displays, notice that **Orlando** displays in bold, indicating it is open in the file list. Then, on the list, click **Honolulu**.

The subfolders within the Honolulu folder display.

5 In the **address bar**, to the right of **win01_1B_Bell_Orchid**, click the ⟩ arrow again to display the subfolders in that folder. Then, on the **address bar**—not on the list—point to **Honolulu** and notice that the list of subfolders in the **Honolulu** folder displays.

After you display one set of subfolders in the address bar, all of the links are active and you need only point to them to display the list of subfolders.

Clicking an arrow to the right of a folder name in the address bar displays a list of the subfolders in that folder. You can click a subfolder name to display its contents. In this manner, the address bar is not only a path, but it is also an active control with which you can step from the current folder directly to any other folder above it in the folder structure just by clicking a folder name.

6 On the list of subfolders for **Honolulu**, click **Sales_Marketing** to display its contents in the **file list**. On the **View tab**, in the **Layout group**, if necessary, click **Details**. Compare your screen with Figure 1.54.

↻ **ANOTHER WAY**   In the file list, double-click the Sales_Marketing folder.

The files in the Sales_Marketing folder for Honolulu display in the Details layout. To the left of each file name, an icon indicates the program that created each file. Here, there is one PowerPoint file, one Excel file, one Word file, and four JPEG images.

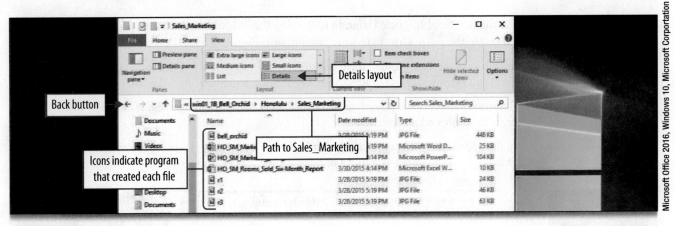

FIGURE 1.54

7 In the upper left portion of the window, click **Back** ⬅ one time.

The Back button retraces each of your clicks in the same manner as clicking the Back button when you are browsing the Internet.

8 In the **file list**, point to the **Human_Resources** folder, and then double-click to open the folder.

9 In the **file list**, click one time to select the PowerPoint file **HO_HR_New_Employee_Presentation**, and then on the ribbon, click the **View tab**. In the **Panes group**, click **Details pane**, and then compare your screen with Figure 1.55.

The *Details pane* displays the most common *file properties* associated with the selected file. File properties refer to information about a file, such as the author, the date the file was last changed, and any descriptive *tags*—properties that you create to help you find and organize your files.

Additionally, a thumbnail image of the first slide in the presentation displays, and the status bar displays the number of items in the folder.

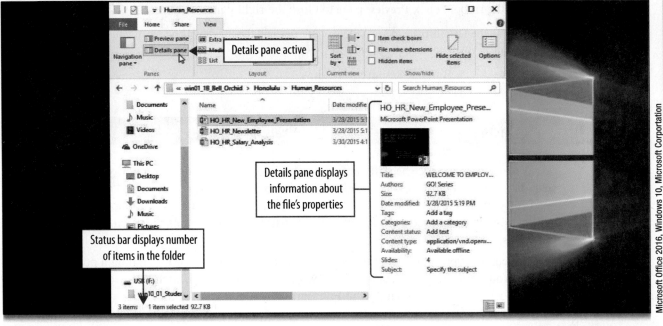

FIGURE 1.55

10 On the right, in the **Details pane**, click **Add a tag**, type **New Employee meeting** and then at the bottom of the pane click **Save**.

You can add tags to files to make them easier to find, because you can search for tags.

🔄 **ANOTHER WAY** With the file selected, on the Home tab, in the Open group, click Properties to display the Properties dialog box for the file.

11 On the ribbon, on the **View tab**, in the **Panes group**, click **Preview pane** to replace the **Details pane** with the **Preview pane**. Compare your screen with Figure 1.56.

In the Preview pane that displays on the right, you can use the scroll bar to scroll through the slides in the presentation; or, you can click the up or down scroll arrow to view the slides as a miniature presentation.

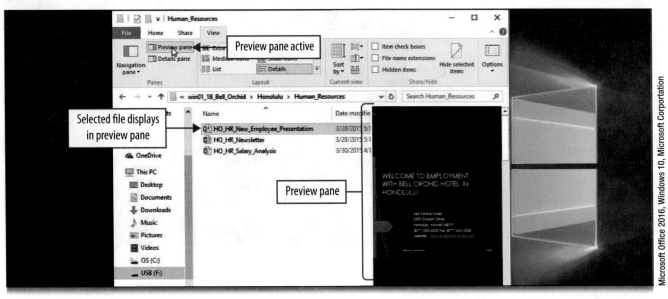

FIGURE 1.56

12 On the ribbon, click **Preview pane** to close the right pane.

Use the Details pane to see a file's properties and the Preview pane when you want to look at a file quickly without actually opening it.

13 **Close** ☒ the **Human_Resources** window.

Objective 9 | Start Programs and Open Data Files

When you are using the software programs installed on your computer, you create and save data files—the documents, workbooks, databases, songs, pictures, and so on that you need for your job or personal use. Therefore, most of your work with Windows 10 desktop applications is concerned with locating and starting your programs and locating and opening your files.

You can start programs from the Start menu or from the taskbar by pinning a program to the taskbar. You can open your data files from within the program in which they were created, or you can open a data file from a window in File Explorer, which will simultaneously start the program and open your file.

Activity 1.23 | Starting Programs

1 Close any open windows. Click **Start** ⊞ to place the insertion point in the search box, and then type **paint** Compare your screen with Figure 1.57.

The Windows 10 search feature will immediately begin searching your PC and the web when you type in the search box. Here, Windows 10 searches your computer for applications and Documents containing the term *paint*, and searches Windows Store apps and the Web for the word *paint*.

Paint is a Windows desktop application that comes with Windows 10 with which you can create and edit drawings and display and edit stored photos.

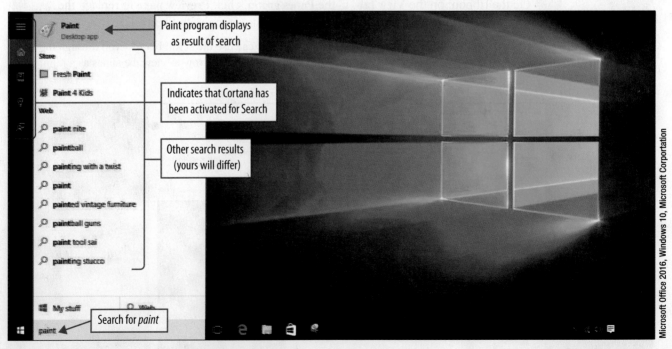

FIGURE 1.57

2 With the **Paint Desktop app** selected—also referred to as *in focus*—as the result of your search, press Enter to open this Windows desktop application.

3 On the ribbon of the Paint program, with the **Home tab** active, in the **Tools group**, click the **Pencil** icon. Move your mouse pointer into the white drawing area, hold down the left mouse button, and then with your mouse, try drawing the letters of your first name in the white area of the window.

 BY TOUCH   Use your finger to draw on the screen.

4 In the upper left corner, to the left of the **Home tab**, click the **File tab** to display a menu of commands for things you can do with your picture.

5 At the bottom of the menu, click **Exit**. In the displayed message, click **Don't Save**.

Messages like this display in most programs to prevent you from forgetting to save your work. A file saved in the Paint program creates a graphic file in the JPEG format.

6 Click **Start** ⊞ to place the insertion point in the search box, type **wordpad** and then open the **WordPad Desktop app**. Notice that this program window has characteristics similar to the Paint program window; for example, it has a ribbon of commands.

7 With the insertion point blinking in the document window, type your first and last name.

8 From the taskbar, start **Snipping Tool**, and then create a **Window Snip**. Click anywhere in the WordPad window to display the **Snipping Tool** mark-up window. **Save** the snip as a **JPEG** in your **Windows 10 Chapter 1** folder as **Lastname_Firstname_1B_WordPad_Snip** Hold this file until you finish this project, and then submit this file as directed by your instructor.

9 **Close** ☒ the **Snipping Tool** window. **Close** ☒ **WordPad**, and then click **Don't Save**.

10 Search for the **windows journal** desktop app and open it—click **Cancel** if asked to install print information. Search for the **alarms & clock** Windows Store app and open it. Search for the **calculator** Windows Store app and open it. Search for **network and sharing center** and open it. Compare your screen with Figure 1.58.

Windows Journal is a desktop app that comes with Windows 10 with which you can type or handwrite—on a touch screen—notes and then store them or email them. The *Network and Sharing Center* is a Windows 10 feature in the Control Panel where you can view your basic network information.

You can open multiple programs and apps, and each one displays in its own window. Each open program displays an icon on the taskbar.

You can see that for both desktop apps that come with Windows 10 and Windows Store apps, the easiest way to find a program is to simply search for it, and then open it from the list of results.

WINDOWS 10

1

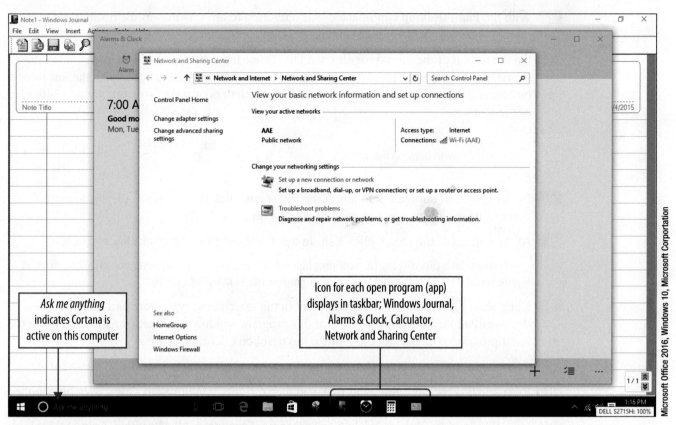

Ask me anything indicates Cortana is active on this computer

Icon for each open program (app) displays in taskbar; Windows Journal, Alarms & Clock, Calculator, Network and Sharing Center

Microsoft Office 2016, Windows 10, Microsoft Corporation

FIGURE 1.58

11 Click **Start** ▦, and then directly above the Start button, click **All apps**. Click the letter **A** to display an onscreen alphabet, and then click **W** to quickly jump to the W section of the list. Click **Windows Accessories**. Compare your screen with Figure 1.59.

These are programs that come with Windows 10. You can open them from this list or search for them as you just practiced. Additionally, use the technique you just practiced to quickly jump to a section of the All apps list without scrolling.

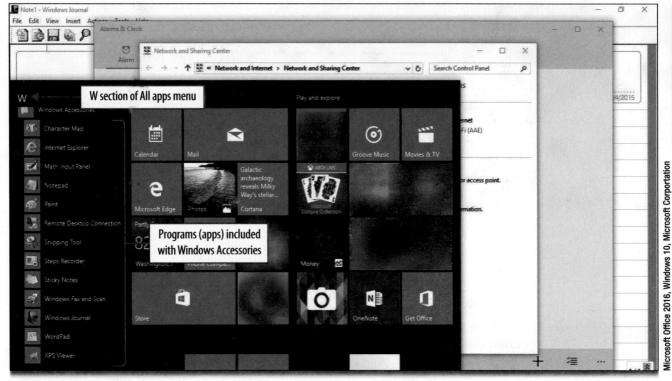

FIGURE 1.59

12 On the taskbar, click the **Windows Journal** icon, and then on the taskbar, click the **Alarms & Clocks** icon.

Use the taskbar to quickly move among open apps.

13 **Close** ⊠ all open windows and redisplay the desktop.

Activity 1.24 | Opening Data Files

> **NOTE** **You Need Microsoft Word 2016 or Word 2013**
>
> For this Project you need Microsoft Word 2016 or Word 2013 on your computer; you can use a trial version if necessary.

1 Click **Start**, type **word 2016** (or type *word 2013* if that is the version of Word on your computer) and then open the **Word** desktop app. Maximize the window if necessary. Compare your screen with Figure 1.60.

The Word program window has features that are common to other programs you have opened; for example, commands are arranged on tabs. When you create and save data in Word, you create a Word document file.

2 On the left, click **Open Other Documents**. Notice the list of places from which you can open a document, including your OneDrive if you are logged in. Click **Browse** to display the **Open** dialog box. Compare your screen with Figure 1.61, and then take a moment to study the table in Figure 1.62.

Recall that a dialog box is a window containing options for completing a task; its layout is similar to that of a File Explorer window. When you are working in a desktop application, use the Open dialog box to locate and open existing files that were created in the desktop application.

When you click Browse, typically the Documents folder on This PC displays. You can use the skills you have practiced to navigate to other locations on your computer, such as your removable USB flash drive.

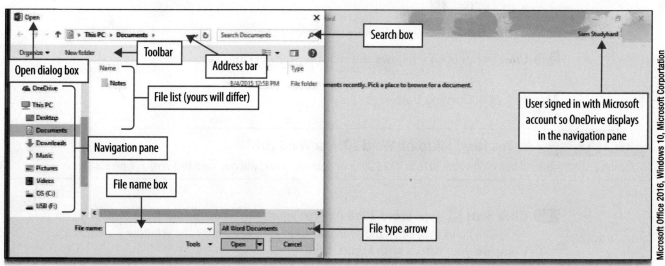

DIALOG BOX ELEMENT	FUNCTION
Address bar	Displays the path in the folder structure.
File list	Displays the list of files and folders that are available in the folder indicated in the address bar.
File name box	Enables you to type the name of a specific file to locate it—if you know it.
File type arrow	Enables you to restrict the type of files displayed in the file list; for example, the default *All Word Documents* restricts (filters) the type of files displayed to only Word documents. You can click the arrow and adjust the restrictions (filters) to a narrower or wider group of files.
Navigation pane	Navigate to files and folders and get access to Quick access, OneDrive, and This PC.
Search box	Search for files in the current folder. Filters the file list based on text that you type; the search is based on text in the file name (and for files on the hard drive or OneDrive, in the file itself), and on other properties that you can specify. The search takes place in the current folder, as displayed in the address bar, and in any subfolders within that folder.
Toolbar	Displays relevant tasks; for example, creating a new folder.

FIGURE 1.62

3 In the **navigation pane**, scroll down as necessary, and then under **This PC**, click your **USB flash drive**. In the **file list**, double-click your **win10_01_Student_Data_Files** folder to open it and display its contents. Then double-click the **win01_1B_Bell_Orchid** folder to open it and display its contents.

4 In the upper right portion of the **Open** dialog box, click the **More options arrow** ▾, and then set the view to **Large icons**. Compare your screen with Figure 1.63.

The Live Preview feature indicates that each folder contains additional subfolders.

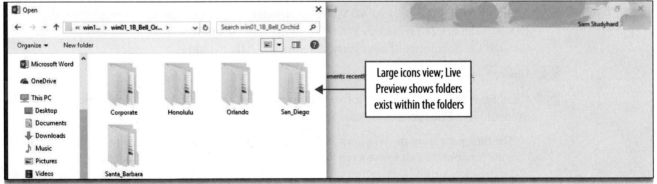

FIGURE 1.63

Microsoft Office 2016, Windows 10, Microsoft Corportation

5 In the **file list**, double-click the **Corporate** folder, and then double-click the **Accounting** folder.

The view returns to the Details view.

6 In the **file list**, notice that only one document—a Word document—displays. In the lower right corner, locate the **File type** button, and notice that *All Word Documents* displays as the file type. Click the **File type arrow**, and then on the displayed list, click **All Files**. Compare your screen with Figure 1.64.

When you change the file type to *All Files*, you can see that the Word file is not the only file in this folder. By default, the Open dialog box displays only the files created in the *active program*; however, you can display variations of file types in this manner.

Microsoft Office file types are identified by small icons, which is a convenient way to differentiate one type of file from another. Although you can view all the files in the folder, you can open only the files that were created in the active program, which in this instance is Microsoft Word.

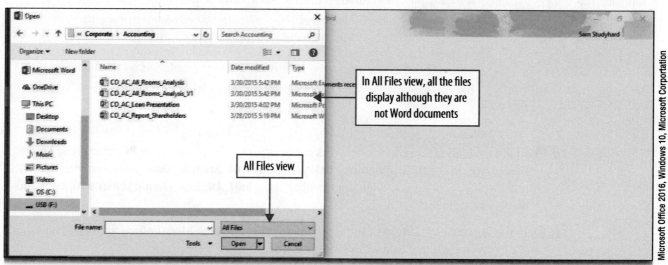

FIGURE 1.64

7 Change the file type back to **All Word Documents**. Then in the **file list**, double-click the **CO_AC_Report_Shareholders** Word file to open the document. Take a moment to scroll through the document. If necessary, Maximize ☐ the window.

8 **Close** ☒ the Word window.

9 Click **Start** ⊞, and then search for **.txt** Open one of the **Structure.txt** files, which are in your Student Data Files several times.

The file opens using the Windows 10 *Notepad* desktop app—a basic text-editing program included with Windows 10 that you can use to create simple documents.

In the search box, you can search for files on your computer, and you can search for a file by its *file name extension*—a set of characters at the end of a file name that helps Windows understand what kind of information is in a file and what program should open it. A *.txt file* is a simple file consisting of lines of text with no formatting and that almost any computer can open and display.

10 **Close** ☒ all open windows.

Storing Files and Creating Desktop Shortcuts for a Program on Your Desktop

On your desktop, you can add or remove *desktop shortcuts*, which are desktop icons that can link to items accessible on your computer such as a program, file, folder, disk drive, printer, or another computer. In previous versions of Windows, many computer users commonly did this.

Now the Start menu is your personal dashboard for all your programs and online activities, and increasingly you will access programs and your own files in the cloud. So do not clutter your desktop with shortcuts—doing so is more confusing than useful. Placing desktop shortcuts for frequently used programs or folders directly on your desktop may seem convenient, but as you add more icons, your desktop becomes cluttered and the shortcuts are not easy to find. A better organizing method is to use the taskbar for shortcuts to programs. For folders and files, the best organizing structure is to create a logical structure of folders within your Documents folder.

You can also drag frequently-used folders to the Quick access area in the navigation pane so that they are available any time you open File Explorer. As you progress in your use of Windows 10, you will discover techniques for using the taskbar and the Quick access area of the navigation pane to streamline your work, instead of cluttering your desktop.

Activity 1.25 | Searching, Pinning, Sorting, and Filtering in File Explorer

1 Click **File Explorer**. On the right, at the bottom, notice that under **Recent files**, you can see files that you have recently opened.

2 In the **navigation pane**, click your **USB flash drive**—or click the location where you have stored your student data files for this Project. In the upper right, click in the **Search** box, and then type **pool** Compare your screen with Figure 1.65.

> Files that contain the word *pool* in the title display. If you are searching a folder on your hard drive or OneDrive, files that contain the word *pool* within the document will also display. Additionally, Search Tools display on the ribbon.

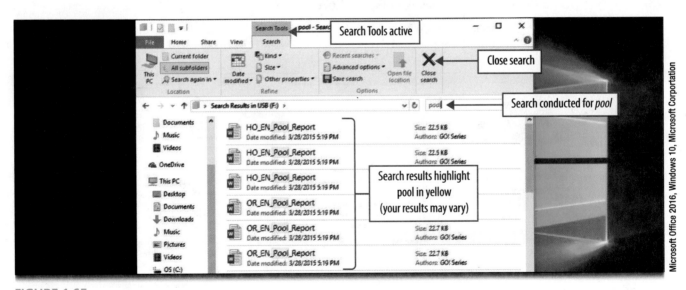

FIGURE 1.65

3 In the search box, clear the search by clicking ☒, and then in the search box type **dogs.jpg** Notice that you can also search by using a file extension as part of the search term.

4 **Clear** ☒ the search. In the **file list**, double-click your **win10_01_Student_Data_Files** folder to open it in the file list, and then click one time on your **win01_1B_Bell_Orchid** folder to select it.

5 On the **Home tab**, in the **Clipboard group**, click **Pin to Quick access**. Compare your screen with Figure 1.66.

You can pin frequently used folders to the Quick access area, and then unpin them when you no longer need frequent access. Folders that you access frequently will also display in the Quick access area without the pin image. Delete them by right-clicking the name and clicking Unpin from Quick access.

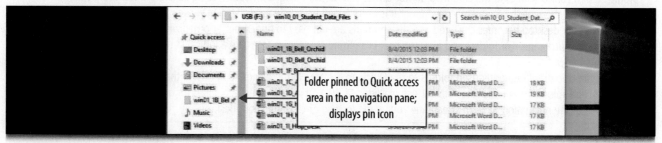

FIGURE 1.66

ANOTHER WAY In the file list, right-click a folder name, and then click Pin to Quick access; or, drag the folder to the Quick access area in the navigation pain and release the mouse button when the ScreenTip displays Pin to Quick access.

6 In the **file list**—or from the Quick access area—double-click your **win01_1B_Bell_Orchid** folder to display its contents in the file list. Double-click the **Corporate** folder and then double-click the **Engineering** folder.

7 Point to an empty area of the **file list**, right-click, point to **Sort by**, and then click **Type**. Compare your screen with Figure 1.67.

Use this technique to sort files in the file list by type. Here, the JPG files display first, and then the Microsoft Excel files, and so on—in alphabetic order by file type.

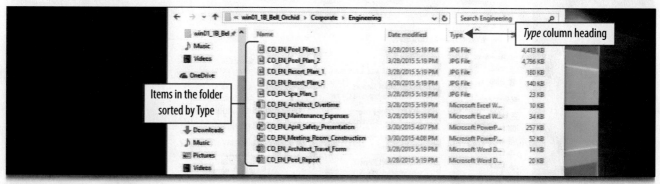

FIGURE 1.67

8 Point to the column heading **Type**, and then click ∧.

9 Point to the column heading **Type** again, and on the right, click ∨. On the displayed list, click **Microsoft PowerPoint Presentation**, and notice that the file list is filtered to show only PowerPoint files.

A *filtered list* is a display of files that is limited based on specified criteria.

10 Click the check box to clear the Microsoft PowerPoint filter and redisplay all of the files.

11 **Close** ⊠ all open windows.

Objective 10 Create, Rename, and Copy Files and Folders

File management includes organizing, copying, naming, renaming, moving, and deleting the files and folders you have stored in various locations—both locally and in the cloud.

Activity 1.26 | Copying Files from a Removable Storage Device to the Documents Folder on the Hard Disk Drive

Barbara and Steven have the assignment to transfer and then organize some of the corporation's files to a computer that will be connected to the corporate network. Data on such a computer can be accessed by employees at any of the hotel locations through the use of sharing technologies. For example, *SharePoint* is a Microsoft technology that enables employees in an organization to access information across organizational and geographic boundaries.

1 ▶ Close any open windows. If necessary, insert the USB flash drive that contains the Student Data Files that accompany this chapter that you downloaded from the Pearson website or obtained from your instructor.

2 ▶ Open **File Explorer** 🗔 . In the **navigation pane**, if necessary expand **This PC**, and then click your USB flash drive to display its contents in the file list.

Recall that in the navigation pane, under This PC, you have access to all the storage areas inside your computer, such as your hard disk drives, and to any devices with removable storage, such as CDs, DVDs, or USB flash drives.

3 ▶ In the **file list**, double-click **win10_01_Student_Data_Files** (not the zipped folder if you still have it) to open it, and then click one time on the **win01_1B_Bell_Orchid** to select the folder. Compare your screen with Figure 1.68.

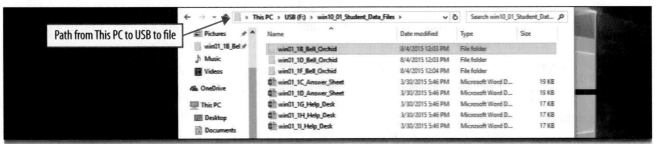

FIGURE 1.68

Microsoft Office 2016, Windows 10, Microsoft Corporation

4 With the **win01_1B_Bell_Orchid** folder on your USB drive selected, on the ribbon, on the **Home tab**, in the **Clipboard group**, click **Copy**.

The Copy command places a copy of your selected file or folder on the *Clipboard* where it will be stored until you use the Paste command to insert the copy somewhere else. The Clipboard is a temporary storage area for information that you have copied or moved from one place and plan to use somewhere else.

In Windows 10, the Clipboard can hold only one piece of information at a time. Whenever something is copied to the Clipboard, it replaces whatever was there before. In Windows 10, you cannot view the contents of the Clipboard nor place multiple items there in the manner that you can in Microsoft Word.

ANOTHER WAY   With the item selected in the file list, press Ctrl + C to copy the item to the clipboard.

5 To the left of the address bar, click **Up** ↑ two times. In the **file list**, double-click your **Documents** folder to open it, and then on the **Home tab**, in the **Clipboard group**, click **Paste**.

A *progress bar* displays in a dialog box, and also displays on the File Explorer taskbar button with green shading. A progress bar indicates visually the progress of a task such as a copy process, a download, or a file transfer.

The Documents folder is one of several folders within your *personal folder* stored on the hard disk drive. For each user account—even if there is only one user on the computer—Windows 10 creates a personal folder labeled with the account holder's name.

ANOTHER WAY   With the destination location selected, press Ctrl + V to paste the item from the clipboard to the selected location. Or, on the Home tab, in the Organize group, click Copy to, find and then click the location to which you want to copy. If the desired location is not on the list, use the Choose location command at the bottom.

6 Close ✕ the **Documents** window.

Activity 1.27 | Creating Folders, Renaming Folders, and Renaming Files

Barbara and Steven can see that various managers have been placing files related to the new European hotels in the *Future_Hotels* folder. They can also see that the files have not been organized into a logical structure. For example, files that are related to each other are not in separate folders; instead they are mixed in with other files that are not related to the topic.

In this activity, you will create, name, and rename folders to begin a logical structure of folders in which to organize the files related to the European hotels project.

1 On the taskbar, click **File Explorer** 📁, and then use any of the techniques you have practiced to display the contents of the **Documents** folder in the **file list**.

NOTE   Using the Documents Folder and OneDrive Instead of Your USB Drive

In this modern computing era, you should limit your use of USB drives to those times when you want to quickly take some files to another computer without going online. Instead of using a USB drive, use your computer's hard drive, or better yet, your free OneDrive cloud storage that comes with your Microsoft account.

There are two good reasons to stop using USB flash drives. First, searching is limited on a USB drive—search does not look at the content inside a file. When you search files on your hard drive or OneDrive, the search extends to words and phrases actually *inside* the files. Second, if you delete a file or folder from a USB drive, it is gone and cannot be retrieved. Files you delete from your hard drive or OneDrive go to the Recycle Bin where you can retrieve them later.

---

2 In the **file list**, double-click the **win01_1B_Bell_Orchid** folder, double-click the **Corporate** folder, double-click the **Information_Technology** folder, and then double-click the **Future_Hotels** folder to display its contents in the file list; sometimes this navigation is written as *Documents > win01_1B_Bell_Orchid > Corporate > Information_Technology > Future_Hotels*.

> Some computer users prefer to navigate a folder structure by double-clicking in this manner. Others prefer using the address bar as described in the following Another Way box. Use whatever method you prefer—double-clicking in the file list, clicking in the address bar, or expanding files in the navigation pane.

ANOTHER WAY   In the navigation pane, click Documents, and expand each folder in the navigation pane. Or, In the address bar, to the right of Documents, click >, and then on the list, click win01_1B_Bell_Orchid. To the right of win01_1B_Bell_Orchid, click > and then click Corporate. To the right of Corporate, click > and then click Information_Technology. To the right of Information_Technology, click >, and then click Future_Hotels.

3 In the **file list**, be sure the items are in alphabetical order by **Name**. If the items are not in alphabetical order, recall that by clicking the small arrow in the column heading name, you can change how the files in the file list are ordered.

4 On the ribbon, click the **View tab**, and then in the **Layout group**, be sure **Details** is selected.

> The *Details view* displays a list of files or folders and their most common properties.

ANOTHER WAY   Right-click in a blank area of the file list, point to View, and then click Details.

5 On the ribbon, click the **Home tab**, and then in the **New group**, click **New folder**. With the text *New folder* selected, type **Paris** and press [Enter]. Click **New folder** again, and then type **Venice** and press [Enter]. Create a third **New folder** named **London**

> In a Windows 10 file list, folders are listed first, in alphabetic order, followed by individual files in alphabetic order.

6 Click the **Venice** folder one time to select it, and then on the ribbon, in the **Organize group**, click **Rename**. Notice that the text *Venice* is selected. Type **Rome** and press [Enter].

ANOTHER WAY   Point to a folder or file name, right-click, and then on the shortcut menu, click Rename.

7 In the **file list**, click one time to select the Word file **Architects**. With the file name selected, click the file name again to select all the text. Click the file name again to place the insertion point within the file name, edit the file name to **Architects_Local** and press [Enter]. Compare your screen with Figure 1.69.

> You can use any of the techniques you just practiced to change the name of a file or folder.

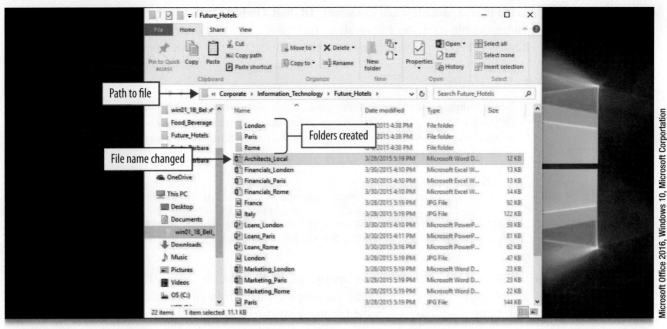

Path to file

Folders created

File name changed

FIGURE 1.69

8 From the taskbar, start **Snipping Tool**; if necessary drag the *title bar*—the bar across the top of a window that displays the program name—of Snipping Tool into a blank area of the desktop. Click the **New arrow**, and then click **Window Snip**. Point anywhere in the **Future_ Hotels** window and click one time. In the **Snipping Tool** mark-up window, click **Save Snip** 🖫.

9 In the **Save As** dialog box, in the **navigation pane**, scroll down as necessary, and then click your USB flash drive so that it displays in the **address bar**.

10 In the **file list**, double-click your **Windows 10 Chapter 1** folder to open it. Click in the **File name** box, and then replace the selected text by typing **Lastname_Firstname_1B_Europe_Folders_Snip**

11 Be sure the file type is **JPEG**. Click **Save** or press Enter. **Close** ✕ the **Snipping Tool** window. Hold this file until you finish this Project.

12 **Close** ✕ all open windows.

Activity 1.28 │ Copying Files

Copying, moving, renaming, and deleting files and folders comprise the most heavily used features within File Explorer. Probably half or more of the steps you complete in File Explorer relate to these tasks, so mastering these techniques will increase your efficiency.

When you *copy* a file or a folder, you make a duplicate of the original item and then store the duplicate in another location. In this activity, you will assist Barbara and Steven in making copies of the Staffing_Plan file and then placing the copies in each of the three folders you created— London, Paris, and Rome.

1 From the taskbar, open **File Explorer** 🗔, and then by double-clicking in the file list or following the links in the address bar, navigate to **This PC > Documents > win01_1B_Bell_Orchid > Corporate > Information_Technology > Future_Hotels**.

2 **Maximize** ▢ the window. On the **View tab**, if necessary set the **Layout** to **Details**, and then in the **Current view group**, click **Size all columns to fit** 🖽.

3 In the **file list**, click the file **Staffing_Plan** one time to select it, and then on the **Home tab**, in the **Clipboard group**, click **Copy**.

4 At the top of the **file list**, double-click the **London folder** to open it, and then in the **Clipboard group**, click **Paste**. Notice that the copy of the **Staffing_Plan** file displays. Compare your screen with Figure 1.70.

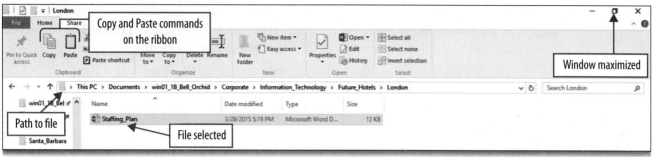

FIGURE 1.70

🔄 **ANOTHER WAY**　　Right-click the file you want to copy, and on the menu click Copy. Then right-click the folder into which you want to place the copy, and on the menu click Paste. Or, select the file you want to copy, press Ctrl + C to activate the Copy command, open the folder into which you want to paste the file, and then press Ctrl + V to activate the Paste command.

---

5 With the **London** window open, by using any of the techniques you have practiced, rename this copy of the **Staffing_Plan** file to **London_Staffing_Plan**

6 To the left of the **address bar**, click **Up** ↑ to move up one level in the folder structure and redisplay the file list for the **Future_Hotels** folder.

🔄 **ANOTHER WAY**　　In the address bar, click Future_Hotels to redisplay this window and move up one level in the folder structure.

---

7 Click the **Staffing_Plan** file one time to select it, hold down Ctrl, and then drag the file upward over the **Paris** folder until the ScreenTip + *Copy to Paris* displays, and then release the mouse button and release Ctrl.

When dragging a file into a folder, holding down Ctrl engages the Copy command and places a *copy* of the file at the location where you release the mouse button. This is another way to copy a file or copy a folder.

8 Open the **Paris** folder, and then rename the **Staffing_Plan** file **Paris_Staffing_Plan** Then, move up one level in the folder structure to display the **Future_Hotels** window.

9 Double-click the **Rome** folder to open it. With your mouse pointer anywhere in the **file list**, right-click, and then from the shortcut menu click **Paste**.

A copy of the Staffing_Plan file is copied to the folder. Because a copy of the Staffing_Plan file is still on the Clipboard, you can continue to paste the item until you copy another item on the Clipboard to replace it.

10 Rename the file **Rome_Staffing_Plan**

11 On the **address bar**, click **Future_Hotels** to move up one level and open the **Future_Hotels** window—or click **Up** ↑ to move up one level. Leave this folder open for the next activity.

Activity 1.29 | Moving Files

When you move a file or folder, you remove it from the original location and store it in a new location. In this Activity, you will move items from the Future_Hotels folder into their appropriate folders.

1 With the **Future_Hotels** folder open, in the **file list**, click the Excel file **Financials_London** one time to select it. On the **Home tab**, in the **Clipboard group**, click **Cut**.

The file's Excel icon dims. This action places the item on the Clipboard.

ANOTHER WAY Right-click the file or folder, and on the shortcut menu, click Cut; or, select the file or folder, and then press Ctrl + X.

2 Double-click the **London** folder to open it, and then on the **Home tab**, in the **Clipboard group**, click **Paste**.

ANOTHER WAY Right-click the folder, and on the shortcut menu, click Paste; or, select the folder, and then press Ctrl + V.

3 Click **Up** ↑ to move up one level and redisplay the **Future_Hotels** folder window. In the **file list**, point to **Financials_Paris**, hold down the left mouse button, and then drag the file upward over the **Paris** folder until the ScreenTip →*Move to Paris* displays, and then release the mouse button.

4 Open the **Paris** folder, and notice that the file was moved to this folder. Click **Up** ↑—or on the address bar, click Future_Hotels to return to that folder.

5 In the **file list**, click **Loans_London**, hold down Ctrl, and then click **London** and **Marketing_London** to select the three files. Release the Ctrl key. Compare your screen with Figure 1.71.

Use this technique to select a group of noncontiguous items in a list.

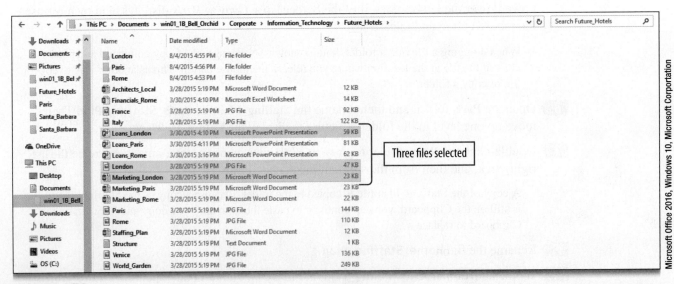

FIGURE 1.71

6 ▸ Point to any of the selected files, hold down the left mouse button, and then drag upward over the **London** folder until the ScreenTip ➔*Move to London* displays and *3* displays over the files being moved, and then release the mouse button.

> You can see that by keeping related files together—for example, all the files that relate to the London hotel—in folders that have an appropriately descriptive name, it will be easier to locate information later.

7 ▸ By dragging, move the **Architects_Local** file into the **London** folder.

8 ▸ In an empty area of the file list, right-click, and then click **Undo Move**. Leave the **Future_Hotels** window open for the next activity.

> Any action that you make in a file list can be undone in this manner.

⟳ ANOTHER WAY   Press Ctrl + Z to undo an action in the file list.

More Knowledge   **Using Shift + Click to Select Files**

If files to be selected are contiguous (next to each other in the file list), click the first file to be selected and then press Shift and click the left mouse button on the last file to select all of the files between the top and bottom file selections.

Activity 1.30 │ Copying and Moving Files by Snapping Two Windows

Sometimes you will want to open, in a second window, another instance of a program that you are using; that is, two copies of the program will be running simultaneously. This capability is especially useful in the File Explorer program, because you are frequently moving or copying files from one location to another.

In this activity, you will open two instances of File Explorer, and then use the *Snap* feature to display both instances on your screen.

To copy or move files or folders into a different level of a folder structure, or to a different drive location, the most efficient method is to display two windows side by side and then use drag and drop or copy (or cut) and paste commands.

In this activity, you will assist Barbara and Steven in making copies of the Staffing_Plan files for the corporate office.

1 ▸ In the upper right corner, click **Restore Down** ⧉ to restore the **Future_Hotels** window to its previous size and not maximized on the screen.

2 ▸ Hold down ⊞ and press ← to snap the window so that it occupies the left half of the screen.

3 ▸ On the taskbar, right-click **File Explorer** ▭, and then on the list, click **File Explorer** to open another instance of the program. With the new window active, hold down ⊞ and press → to snap the window so that it occupies the right half of the screen.

⟳ ANOTHER WAY   Drag the title bar of a window to the left or right side of the screen and when your mouse pointer reaches the edge, it will snap it into place.

4 ▸ In the window on the right, click in a blank area to make the window active. Then navigate to **Documents > win01_1B_Bell_Orchid > Corporate > Human_Resources**. Compare your screen with Figure 1.72.

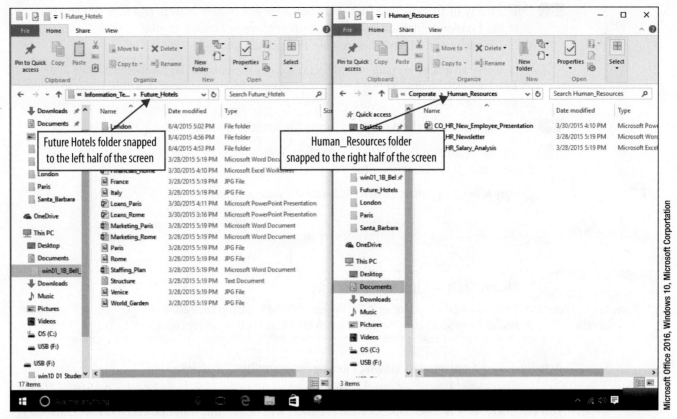

Future Hotels folder snapped
to the left half of the screen

Human_Resources folder
snapped to the right half of the screen

FIGURE 1.72

5 In the left window, double-click to open the **Rome** folder, and then click one time to select the file **Rome_Staffing_Plan**.

6 Hold down `Ctrl`, and then drag the file into the right window, into an empty area of the **Human_Resources file list**, until the ScreenTip + *Copy to Human_Resources* displays and then release the mouse button and `Ctrl`.

7 In the left window, on the **address bar**, click **Future_Hotels** to redisplay that folder. Open the **Paris** folder, point to **Paris_Staffing_Plan** and right-click, and then click **Copy**.

> You can access the Copy command in various ways; for example, from the shortcut menu, on the ribbon, or by using the keyboard shortcut `Ctrl` + `C`.

8 In the right window, point anywhere in the **file list**, right-click, and then click **Paste**.

9 Start the **Snipping Tool** program, click the **New arrow**, and then click **Full-screen Snip**. In the **Snipping Tool** mark-up window, click **Save Snip** 💾.

10 In the displayed **Save As** dialog box, notice the path in the **address bar**. If necessary, in the navigation pane, under **This PC**, click your USB flash drive, and then display the window for your **Windows 10 Chapter 1** folder.

11 Be sure the file type is **JPEG**. Using your own name, as the file name type **Lastname_Firstname_1B_HR_Snip** and press `Enter`. Hold this file until you have completed this Project.

12 **Close** ✕ all open windows.

Microsoft Office 2016, Windows 10, Microsoft Corportation

Activity 1.31 │ Deleting Files and Using the Recycle Bin

It is good practice to delete files and folders that you no longer need from your hard disk drive and removable storage devices. Doing so makes it easier to keep your data organized and also frees up storage space.

When you delete a file or folder from any area of your computer's hard disk drive or from OneDrive, the file or folder is not immediately deleted. Instead, the deleted item is stored in the *Recycle Bin* and remains there until the Recycle Bin is emptied. Thus, you can recover an item deleted from your computer's hard disk drive or OneDrive so long as the Recycle Bin has not been emptied. Items deleted from removable storage devices like a USB flash drive and from some network drives are immediately deleted and cannot be recovered from the Recycle Bin.

To permanently delete a file without first moving it to the Recycle Bin, click the item, hold down Shift, and then press Del. A message will display indicating *Are you sure you want to permanently delete this file?* Use caution when using Shift + Del to permanently delete a file because this action is not reversible.

You can restore items by dragging them from the file list of the Recycle Bin window to the file list of the folder window in which you want to restore them. Or, you can restore them to the location from which they were deleted by right-clicking the items in the file list of the Recycle Bin window and selecting Restore.

Self-Check │ Answer These Questions to Check Your Understanding

1 When you delete a file or folder from any area of your computer's hard disk drive or from OneDrive, the file or folder is not deleted; it is automatically stored in the _____ _____.

2 Files deleted from the computer's hard drive or OneDrive can be recovered from the Recycle Bin until the Recycle Bin is _____.

3 Items deleted from removable storage devices such as a USB flash drive are immediately deleted and cannot be _____ from the Recycle Bin.

4 You can permanently delete a file from the hard drive or OneDrive without first moving it to the Recycle Bin, but a warning message will indicate *Are you sure you want to _____ delete this file?*

5 To restore items from the Recycle Bin to the location from which they were deleted, right-click the items and then click _____.

Objective 11 Use OneDrive as Cloud Storage

OneDrive is Microsoft's *cloud storage* product. Cloud storage means that your data is stored on a remote server that is maintained by a company so that you can access your files from anywhere and from any device. The idea of having all of your data on a single device—your desktop or laptop PC—has become old fashioned. Because cloud storage from large companies like Microsoft is secure, many computer users now store their information on cloud services like OneDrive. Anyone with a Microsoft account has a large amount of free storage on OneDrive, and if you have an Office 365 account—free to many college students if your college offers such a program—you have 1 terabyte or more of OneDrive storage that you can use across all Microsoft products. That amount of storage is probably all you will ever need—even if you store lots of photos on your OneDrive.

OneDrive is no longer just an app, as it was in Windows 8. Rather, OneDrive is integrated into the Windows 10 operating system. Similarly, Google's cloud storage called *Google Drive* is integrated into its Chrome operating system, and Apple's cloud storage called *iCloud* is integrated into both the Mac and iOS operating systems.

Activity 1.32 | Using OneDrive as Cloud Storage

When you install Windows 10 or use it for the first time, you will be prompted to set up your OneDrive. The setup process involves determining which folders—if not all—that you want to *sync* to OneDrive. Syncing—also called synchronizing—is the process of updating OneDrive data to match any updates you make on your device, and vice versa. This setup is optional, and you can always come back to it later. Your OneDrive storage, however, will be available from the navigation pane in File Explorer. Additionally, you will always have instant access to your OneDrive from any web browser.

1 **Close** ⨉ any open windows. From the taskbar, start **File Explorer** 📁 and then navigate to **Documents > win01_1B_Bell_Orchid > Santa_Barbara > Sales_Marketing > Media**.

2 Hold down Ctrl, click **Scenic1** and **Scenic2**, and then release Ctrl. With the two files selected, press Ctrl + C, which is the keyboard shortcut for the Copy command.

Although you see no screen action, the two files are copied to the Clipboard.

3 In the **navigation pane**, click **OneDrive**. If a dialog box regarding Customizing your OneDrive settings displays, in the lower right corner, click Cancel.

If you have decided on syncing options, you can do so in this dialog box; or, postpone these decisions by clicking Cancel.

Your OneDrive folders display in the file list.

4 On the ribbon, on the **Home tab**, in the **New group**, click **New folder**. Name the new folder **Marketing Photos** and then press Enter. Double-click the new folder to open it.

5 Press Ctrl + V, which is the keyboard shortcut for the Paste command, to paste the two photos into the folder. On the **View tab**, set the **Layout** to **Details**. Compare your screen with Figure 1.73.

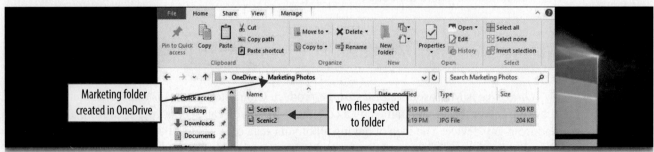

FIGURE 1.73

Microsoft Office 2016, Windows 10, Microsoft Corportation

6 Using the techniques you have practiced, create a window snip and save the snip in your chapter folder. Be sure the file type is **JPEG**. Using your own name, as the file name type **Lastname_Firstname_1B_OneDrive_Snip** and press Enter.

7 **Close** ⨉ all open windows.

END | You have completed Project 1B

END OF CHAPTER

SUMMARY

Windows 10 is optimized for touchscreens and also works with a mouse and keyboard. You will probably use touch when you are reading or communicating on the web and a keyboard when creating files.

The Windows 10 Start menu is your connected dashboard—this is your one-screen view of information that updates continuously with new information and personal communications that are important to you.

The Windows Store apps you use from the Start menu display in separate Windows, similar to your other files, so you can move them on the desktop or display them side by side. These apps typically have a single purpose.

File Explorer is at work anytime you are viewing the contents of a location, a folder, or a file. Use File Explorer to navigate your Windows 10 structure that stores and organizes the files you create.

GO! LEARN IT ONLINE

Review the concepts and key terms in this chapter by completing these online challenges, which you can find in **MyITLab**.

Matching and Multiple Choice: Answer matching and multiple choice questions to test what you learned in this chapter.

Crossword Puzzle: Spell out the words that match the numbered cues, and put them in the puzzle squares.

GO! FOR JOB SUCCESS

Video: Email Etiquette

Your instructor may assign this video to your class, and then ask you to think about, or discuss with your classmates, these questions:

FotolEdhar/Fotolia

Why do you think it is important to follow specific etiquette when composing email?

Why is it important to include a greeting and sign every email you send?

What are the differences between sending a business email and a personal email, and what are three specific things you should never do in a business email?

Project	Apply Skills from These Chapter Objectives	Project Type	Project Location
1C	Objectives 1-6 from Project 1A	**1C Chapter Review** A guided review of the skills from Project 1A.	On the following pages
1D	Objectives 7-11 from Project 1B	**1D Chapter Review** A guided review of the skills from Project 1B.	On the following pages
1E	Objectives 1-6 from Project 1A	**1E Mastery**　　　　　　　**Mastery and Transfer of Learning** A demonstration of your mastery of the skills in Project 1A with decision-making.	On the following pages
1F	Objectives 7-11 from Project 1B	**1F Mastery**　　　　　　　**Mastery and Transfer of Learning** A demonstration of your mastery of the skills in Project 1B with decision-making.	On the following pages
1G	Combination of Objectives from Projects 1A and 1B	**1G GO! Think**　　　　　　　　　　**Critical Thinking** A demonstration of your understanding of the chapter concepts applied in a manner that you would outside of college. An analytic rubric helps you and your instructor grade the quality of your work by comparing it to the work an expert in the discipline would create.	On the following pages
1H	Combination of Objectives from Projects 1A and 1B	**1H GO! Think**　　　　　　　　　　**Critical Thinking** A demonstration of your understanding of the chapter concepts applied in a manner that you would outside of college. An analytic rubric helps you and your instructor grade the quality of your work by comparing it to the work an expert in the discipline would create.	On the following pages
1I	Combination of Objectives from Projects 1A and 1B	**1I GO! Think**　　　　　　　　　　**Critical Thinking** A demonstration of your understanding of the chapter concepts applied in a manner that you would outside of college. An analytic rubric helps you and your instructor grade the quality of your work by comparing it to the work an expert in the discipline would create.	On the following pages

Table caption (top): **Review and Assessment Guide for Windows 10 Chapter 1**

GLOSSARY

GLOSSARY OF CHAPTER KEY TERMS

.png An image file format, commonly pronounced *PING*, that stands for Portable Network Graphic; this is an image file type that can be transferred over the Internet.

.txt file A simple file consisting of lines of text with no formatting that almost any computer can open and display.

Action Center A vertical panel that displays on the right side of your screen when you click the icon in the notifications area of the taskbar; the upper portion displays notifications you have elected to receive such as mail and social network updates and the lower portion displays buttons for frequently used system commands.

Address bar (File Explorer) The area at the top of a File Explorer window that displays your current location in the folder structure as a series of links separated by arrows.

Administrator account A user account that lets you make changes that will affect other users of the computer; the most powerful of the three types of accounts, because it permits the most control over the computer.

All apps A command that displays all the apps installed on your computer in alphabetical order on the Start menu.

App The shortened version of the term *application*, and which typically refers to a smaller application designed for a single purpose.

App bar A term used to describe a horizontal or vertical array of command icons in a Windows app.

Application A set of instructions that a computer uses to accomplish a task; also called a program.

Application developer An individual who writes computer applications.

Badge An icon that displays on the Lock screen for lock screen apps that you have selected.

Bing Microsoft's search engine, which powers Cortana.

Booting the computer The process of turning on a computer when the computer has been completely shut down and during which the BIOS program will run.

Click The action of pressing the left mouse button.

Clipboard A temporary storage area for information that you have copied or moved from one place and plan to use somewhere else.

Cloud storage Storage space on an Internet site that may also display as a drive on your computer.

Compressed file A file that has been reduced in size and that takes up less storage space and can be transferred to other computers faster than uncompressed files.

Compressed Folder Tools File Explorer tools, available on the ribbon, to assist you in extracting compressed files.

Contextual tab A context-sensitive menu that displays commands and options relevant to the active object.

Control Panel An area of Windows 10 where you can manipulate some of the Windows 10 basic system settings—a carryover from previous versions of Windows.

Cortana Microsoft's intelligent personal assistant that is part of the Windows 10 operating system.

Dashboard A descriptive term for the Windows 10 Start menu because it provides a one-screen view of links to information and programs that matter most to the signed-in user.

Data All the files—documents, spreadsheets, pictures, songs, and so on—that you create and store during the day-to-day use of your computer.

Data management The process of managing your files and folders in an organized manner so that you can find information when you need it.

Desktop The main Windows 10 screen that serves as a starting point and surface for your work, like the top of an actual desk.

Desktop app A computer program that is installed on the hard drive of a personal computer and that requires a computer operating system like Microsoft Windows or Apple OSX to run.

Desktop background Displays the colors and graphics of your desktop; you can change the desktop background to look the way you want.

Desktop shortcuts Desktop icons that link to any item accessible on your computer or on a network, such as a program, file, folder, disk drive, printer, or another computer.

Details pane Displays the most common properties associated with the selected file.

Details view A view in File Explorer that displays a list of files or folders and their most common properties.

Dialog box A small window that displays options for completing a task.

Double-click The action of pressing the left mouse button twice in rapid succession while holding the mouse still.

Download The action of transferring or copying a file from another location—such as a cloud storage location or from an Internet site—to your computer.

Downloads folder A folder that holds items that you have downloaded from the Internet.

Drag The action of moving something from one location on the screen to another while holding down the left mouse button; the action of dragging includes releasing the mouse button at the desired time or location.

Drive An area of storage that is formatted with a file system compatible with your operating system and is identified by a drive letter.

Extract The action of decompressing—pulling out—files from a compressed form.

File A collection of information that is stored on a computer under a single name, for example, a text document, a picture, or a program.

File Explorer window A window that displays the contents of the current location and contains helpful parts so that you can navigate within the file organizing structure of Windows.

File History A backup and recovery tool that automatically backs up your files to a separate location.

File list Displays the contents of the current folder or location; if you type text into the Search box, only the folders and files that match your search will display here—including files in subfolders.

File name extension A set of characters at the end of a file name that helps Windows 10 understand what kind of information is in a file and what program should open it.

File properties Information about a file such as its author, the date the file was last changed, and any descriptive tags.

Filtered list A display of files that is limited based on specified criteria.

Folder A container in which you store files.

Folder structure The hierarchy of folders in Windows 10.

Free-form snip When using Snipping Tool, the type of snip that lets you draw an irregular line, such as a circle, around an area of the screen.

Full-screen snip When using Snipping Tool, the type of snip that captures the entire screen.

Get Started A feature in Windows 10 to learn about all the things that Windows 10 can do for you.

Google Drive Google's cloud storage.

Graphical user interface The system by which you interact with your computer and which uses graphics such as an image of a file folder or wastebasket that you click to activate the item represented.

GUI The acronym for a graphical user interface, pronounced *GOO-ee*.

Hamburger Another name for the hamburger menu.

Hamburger menu An icon made up of three lines that evoke a hamburger on a bun.

Hard disk drive The primary storage device located inside your computer and where most of your files and programs are typically stored; usually labeled as drive C.

Hierarchy An arrangement where items are ranked and where each level is lower in rank than the item above it.

HoloLens A see-through holographic computer developed by Microsoft.

Hub A feature in Microsoft Edge where you can save favorite websites and create reading lists.

iCloud Apple's cloud storage that is integrated into its Mac and iOS operating systems.

Icons Small images that represent commands, files, or other windows.

Insertion point A blinking vertical line that indicates where text or graphics will be inserted.

Internet of Things A growing network of physical objects that will have sensors connected to the Internet.

IoT The common acronym for the Internet of Things.

JPEG An acronym for Joint Photographic Experts Group, and which is a common file type used by digital cameras and computers to store digital pictures; JPEG is popular because it can store a high-quality picture in a relatively small file.

Jump list A list that displays when you right-click a button on the taskbar, and which displays locations (in the upper portion) and tasks (in the lower portion) from a program's taskbar button.

Keyboard shortcut A combination of two or more keyboard keys, used to perform a task that would otherwise require a mouse.

Live tiles Tiles on the Windows 10 Start menu that are constantly updated with fresh information relevant to the signed-in user; for example, the number of new email messages, new sports scores of interest, or new updates to social networks such as Facebook or Twitter.

Location Any disk drive, folder, or other place in which you can store files and folders.

Lock screen The first screen that displays after turning on a Windows 10 device and that displays the time, day, and date, and one or more icons representing the status of the device's Internet connection, battery status on a tablet or laptop, and any lock screen apps that are installed such as email notifications.

Lock screen apps Apps that display on a Windows 10 lock screen and that show quick status and notifications, even if the screen is locked.

Maximize The command to display a window in full-screen view.

Menu A list of commands within a category.

Menu bar A group of menus.

Menu icon Another name for the hamburger menu.

Microsoft account A single login account for Microsoft systems and services.

Microsoft Edge The web browser program included with Windows 10.

Mobile device platform The hardware and software environment for smaller-screen devices such as tablets and smartphones.

Mouse pointer Any symbol that displays on your screen in response to moving your mouse.

Navigate Explore within the file organizing structure of Windows 10.

Navigation pane The area on the left side of a folder window in File Explorer that displays the Quick Access area and an expandable list of drives and folders.

Network and Sharing Center A Windows 10 feature in the Control Panel where you can view your basic network information.

Notepad A basic text-editing program included with Windows 10 that you can use to create simple documents.

OneDrive A free file storage and file sharing service provided by Microsoft when you sign up for a free Microsoft account.

Operating system A specific type of computer program that manages the other programs on a computer—including computer devices such as desktop computers, laptop computers, smartphones, tablet computers, and game consoles.

Parent folder In the file organizing structure of File Explorer, the location where the folder you are viewing is saved—one level up in the hierarchy.

Path A sequence of folders (directories) that leads to a specific file or folder.

PC Reset A backup and recovery tool that returns your PC to the condition it was in the day you purchased it.

Pen A pen-shaped stylus that you tap on a computer screen.

Personal folder A folder created for each user account on a Windows 10 computer, labeled with the account holder's name, and which contains the subfolders *Documents, Pictures, Music*.

PIN Acronym for personal identification number; in Windows 10 Settings, you can create a PIN to use in place of a password.

Platform An underlying computer system on which application programs can run.

Point to The action of moving the mouse pointer over a specific area.

Pointer Any symbol that displays on your screen in response to moving your mouse and with which you can select objects and commands.

Pointing device A mouse, touchpad, or other device that controls the pointer position on the screen.

Program A set of instructions that a computer uses to accomplish a task; also called an application.

Progress bar In a dialog box or taskbar button, a bar that indicates visually the progress of a task such as a download or file transfer.

Quick access The navigation pane area in File Explorer where you can pin folders you use frequently and that also adds folders you are accessing frequently.

Quick Access Toolbar (File Explorer) The small row of buttons in the upper left corner of a File Explorer window from which you can perform frequently used commands.

Recently added On the Start menu, a section that displays apps that you have recently downloaded and installed.

Rectangular snip When using Snipping Tool, the type of snip that lets you draw a precise box by dragging the mouse pointer around an area of the screen to form a rectangle.

Recycle Bin A folder that stores anything that you delete from your computer, and from which anything stored there can be retrieved until the contents are permanently deleted by activating the Empty Recycle Bin command.

Removable storage device A portable device on which you can store files, such as a USB flash drive, a flash memory card, or an external hard drive, commonly used to transfer information from one computer to another.

Resources A term used to refer collectively to the parts of your computer such as the central processing unit (CPU), memory, and any attached devices such as a printer.

Restore Down A command to restore a window to its previous size before it was maximized.

Ribbon The area at the top of a folder window in File Explorer that groups common tasks such as copying and moving, creating new folders, emailing and zipping items, and changing views on related tabs.

Right-click The action of clicking the right mouse button.

Screenshot Another name for a screen capture.

ScreenTip Useful information that displays in a small box on the screen when you perform various mouse actions, such as pointing to screen elements.

Scroll arrow An arrow at the top, bottom, left, or right, of a scroll bar that when clicked, moves the window in small increments.

Scroll bar A bar that displays on the bottom or right side of a window when the contents of a window are not completely visible; used to move the window up, down, left, or right to bring the contents into view.

Scroll box The box in a vertical or horizontal scroll bar that you drag to reposition the document on the screen.

Select To specify, by highlighting, a block of data or text on the screen with the intent of performing some action on the selection.

SharePoint A Microsoft technology that enables employees in an organization to access information across organizational and geographic boundaries.

Shortcut menu A context-sensitive menu that displays commands and options relevant to the active object.

Shut down Turning off your computer in a manner that closes all open programs and files, closes your network connections, stops the hard disk, and discontinues the use of electrical power.

Sleep Turning off your computer in a manner that automatically saves your work, stops the fan, and uses a small amount of electrical power to maintain your work in memory.

Snap Assist The ability to drag windows to the edges or corners of your screen, and then having Task View display thumbnails of other open windows so that you can select what other windows you want to snap into place.

Snip The image captured using Snipping Tool.

Snipping Tool A program included with Windows 10 with which you can capture an image of all or part of a computer screen, and then annotate, save, copy, or share the image via email.

Split button A button that has two parts—a button and an arrow; clicking the main part of the button performs a command and clicking the arrow opens a menu with choices.

Start menu The menu that displays when you click the Start button, which consists of a list of installed programs on the left and a customizable group of app tiles on the right.

Subfolder A folder within another folder.

System image backup A backup and recovery tool that creates a full system image backup from which you can restore your entire PC.

System tray Another name for the notification area on the taskbar.

Tags A property that you create and add to a file to help you find and organize your files.

Taskbar The area of the desktop that contains program buttons, and buttons for all open programs; by default, it is located at the bottom of the desktop, but you can move it.

This PC An area on the navigation pane that provides navigation to your internal storage and attached storage devices including optical media such as a DVD drive.

Thumbnail A reduced image of a graphic.

Tiles Square and rectangular boxes on the Windows 10 Start menu from which you can access apps, websites, programs, and tools for using the computer by simply clicking or tapping them.

Title bar The bar across the top of the window that displays the program name.

Universal apps Windows apps that use a common code base to deliver the app to any Windows device.

Unzip Extracting files.

User account A collection of information that tells Windows 10 what files and folders the account holder can access, what changes the account holder can make to the computer system, and what the account holder's personal preferences are.

Virtual desktop An additional desktop display to organize and quickly access groups of windows.

Wallpaper Another term for the desktop background.

Web browser Software with which you display webpages and navigate the Internet.

Window snip When using Snipping Tool, the type of snip that captures the entire displayed window.

Windows 10 An operating system developed by Microsoft Corporation designed to work with mobile computing devices of all types and also with traditional PCs.

Windows apps Apps that run not only on a Windows phone and a Windows tablet, but also on your Windows desktop PC.

Windows Defender Protection built into Windows 10 that helps prevent viruses, spyware, and malicious or unwanted software from being installed on your PC without your knowledge.

Windows Firewall Protection built into Windows 10 that can prevent hackers or malicious software from gaining access to your computer through a network or the Internet.

Windows Journal A desktop app that comes with Windows 10 with which you can type or handwrite—on a touchscreen—notes and then store them or email them.

Windows Store The program where you can find and download Windows apps.

Work access A Windows 10 feature with which you can connect to your work or school system based on established policies.

Zip Compressing files.

Apply 1A skills from these Objectives:

1 Explore the Windows 10 Environment

2 Use File Explorer and Desktop Apps to Create a New Folder and Save a File

3 Identify the Functions of the Windows 10 Operating System

4 Discover Windows 10 Features

5 Sign Out of Windows 10, Turn Off Your Computer, and Manage User Accounts

6 Manage Your Windows 10 System

Skills Review Project 1C Exploring Windows 10

 PROJECT FILES

For Project 1C, you will need the following files:

Your USB flash drive—or other location—containing the student data files

win01_1C_Answer_Sheet (Word document)

You will save your file as:

Lastname_Firstname_1C_Answer_Sheet

1 Close all open windows. On the taskbar, click **File Explorer**, navigate to the location where you are storing your student data files for this chapter, and then open the file **win01_1C_Answer_Sheet**. If necessary, at the top click Enable editing; be sure the window is maximized.

In the upper left corner, click **File**, click **Save As**, click **Browse**, and then navigate to your **Windows 10 Chapter 1** folder. Using your own name, save the document as **Lastname_Firstname_1C_Answer_Sheet**

With the Word document displayed, on the taskbar, click the **Word** button to minimize the window and leave your Word document accessible from the taskbar. **Close** the **File Explorer** window. As you complete each step in this project, write the letter of your answer on a piece of paper; you will fill in your Answer Sheet after you complete all the steps in this project.

Click **Start**, and then with the insertion point blinking in the search box, type **lock screen** Which of the following is true?

A. Search terms that include the text *lock screen* display in the search results.

B. The System settings dialog opens on the desktop.

C. From this screen, you can remove or change your lock screen picture from your computer.

2 At the top of the search results, click **Lock screen settings**. What is your result?

A. Your lock screen picture fills the screen.

B. The PERSONALIZATION window displays with Background selected on the left.

C. The PERSONALIZATION window displays with Lock screen selected on the left.

3 Close the **Settings** window. Click **Start**, click **All apps**, scroll to the **G** section, click **Get Started**, and then on the left, click **Windows Hello**. According to this information, which of the following is true?

A. You cannot activate Windows Hello by using a fingerprint.

B. Windows Hello enables you to sign in to your computer without typing a password.

C. To set up Windows Hello, you must open a Windows Store app.

4 Close the **Get Started** window. On the taskbar, click **File Explorer**. What is your result?

A. The window for your USB flash drive displays.

B. The File Explorer window displays.

C. The Documents window displays.

(Project 1C Exploring Windows 10 continues on the next page)

5 On **This PC**, locate and open **Documents**. What is your result?

A. The first document in the folder opens in its application.

B. The contents of the Documents folder display in the file list.

C. The contents of the Documents folder display in the address bar.

6 In the **navigation pane**, click **This PC**. What is your result?

A. The storage devices attached to your computer display in the file list.

B. All of the files on the hard drive display in the file list.

C. Your computer restarts.

7 **Close** the **This PC** window. Click **Start**, and then in the search box, type **paint** Open the **Paint desktop app**, and then pin the program to the taskbar. **Close** the **Paint** window. Which of the following is true?

A. On the taskbar, the Paint program icon on the taskbar displays with shading and a white line under it.

B. The Paint program tile displays on the right side of the Start menu.

C. The Paint program icon displays on the taskbar with no shading.

8 On the taskbar, point to the **Paint** button, right-click, and then click **Unpin this program from taskbar**. Click **Start**, type **store** and then with the **Store app** at the top of the search results, press Enter. What is your result?

A. All the storage devices attached to your computer display on the Start menu.

B. The Store app displays.

C. A list of games that you can download displays.

9 **Close** the **Store** app. Click **Start**, type **maps** and press Enter; if necessary, enable your current location. Click **Start**, type **weather** and then press Enter. On the taskbar, click **Task View**. What is your result?

A. The Start menu displays.

B. The Weather app opens and fills the screen.

C. All the open apps display as smaller images.

10 Point to the **Weather** app, and then click its **Close** button. In the same manner, close the **Maps** app. What is your result?

A. Your Word document displays as a small image on the desktop.

B. The search results for *Weather* redisplay.

C. The Start menu displays.

To complete this project: On the taskbar, click the Word icon to redisplay your Word document. Type your answers into the correct boxes. Save and close your Word document, and submit as directed by your instructor. **Close** all open windows.

END | You have completed Project 1C

Apply 1B skills from these Objectives:

7 Download and Extract Files and Folders

8 Use File Explorer to Display Locations, Folders, and Files

9 Start Programs and Open Data Files

10 Create, Rename, and Copy Files and Folders

11 Use OneDrive as Cloud Storage

Skills Review Project 1D Working with Windows, Programs, and Files

 PROJECT FILES

For Project 1D, you will need the following files:

Your USB flash drive—or other location—containing the student data files
win01_1D_Answer_Sheet (Word document)

You will save your file as:

Lastname_Firstname_1D_Answer_Sheet

1 Close all open windows. On the taskbar, click **File Explorer**, navigate to the location where you are storing your student data files for this chapter, and then open the file **win01_1D_Answer_Sheet**. If necessary, at the top click Enable Editing; be sure the window is maximized.

In the upper left corner, click **File**, click **Save As**, click **Browse**, and then navigate to your **Windows 10 Chapter 1** folder. Using your own name, save the document as **Lastname_Firstname_1D_Answer_Sheet**

With the Word document displayed, on the taskbar, click the **Word** button to minimize the window and leave your Word document accessible from the taskbar. **Close** the **File Explorer** window. As you complete each step in this project, write the letter of your answer on a piece of paper; you will fill in your Answer Sheet after you complete all the steps in this project.

Open **File Explorer**, navigate to your student data files, and then open your **win01_1D_Bell_Orchid** folder. If necessary, on the **View tab**, set the **Layout** to **Details**.

In the **file list**, how many *folders* display?

A. Four

B. Five

C. Six

2 Navigate to **Corporate ▸ Food_Beverage**. If necessary, change the view to **Details**. How many *folders* are in the **Food_Beverage** folder?

A. Three

B. Two

C. One

3 Open the **Restaurants** folder, and then click one time to select the file **Breakfast_Continental**. On the ribbon, click the **Home tab**. In which group of commands can you change the name of this file?

A. New

B. Select

C. Organize

(Project 1D Working with Windows, Programs, and Files continues on the next page)

Project 1D Working with Windows, Programs, and Files (continued)

4 With the **Breakfast_Continental** file still selected, point to the file name and right-click. Which of the following is *not* true?

A. From this menu, you can rename the file.

B. From this menu, you can print the file.

C. From this menu, you can move the folder to another folder within Corporate.

5 Click on the desktop to close the shortcut menu, and then click the **Up** button to move up one level in the hierarchy and display the file list for the **Food_Beverage** folder. On the ribbon, click the **View tab**. In the **Layout group**, click **Large icons**. What is your result?

A. The window fills the entire screen.

B. Files that are pictures are visible as pictures.

C. Only picture files display in the file list.

6 On the **View tab**, return the **Layout** to **Details**. In the **file list**, click one time to select the file **CO_FB_Menu_Presentation**. In the **Panes group**, click the **Details pane** button. (*Hint*: You can point to a button to see its ScreenTip). By looking at the displayed details about this file on the right, which of the following is an information item you can determine about this file?

A. The number of words on each slide

B. The number of slides in the presentation

C. The slide layout used in the title slide

7 In the **Panes group**, click **Preview pane**. In the **Preview pane**, *slowly* drag the scroll box to the bottom of the scroll bar. Which of the following is *not* true?

A. The slide title displays as you drag the scroll box.

B. The PowerPoint program opens as you drag the scroll box.

C. The slide number displays as you drag the scroll box.

8 On the ribbon, click **Preview pane** to turn off the display of the pane. Point to an empty area of the **file list**, right-click, point to **Sort by**, and then click **Type**. In the Type column, if necessary, click the arrow so that the column is sorted in ascending order. Which of the following is true?

A. The Restaurants folder displays at the bottom of the list.

B. The files are in alphabetic order by name.

C. The files are in alphabetic order by Type.

9 In the **Corporate ▸ Food_Beverage** folder, create a new folder named **Dining_Rooms** Select the three JPG files, and then move them into the new folder. Which of the following is true?

A. The status bar indicates that there are five items in the current folder.

B. The three JPG files display in the file list for Food_Beverage.

C. The Dining_Rooms folder is selected.

(Project 1D Working with Windows, Programs, and Files continues on the next page)

10 Open the **Restaurants** folder, and then in the upper right portion of the window, in the **search** box, type **sales** and press Enter. How many files display with the word *Sales* in the document name?

   A. Three

   B. Four

   C. Five

To complete this project: Close all open windows. On the taskbar, click the Word icon to redisplay your Word document. Type your answers into the correct boxes. Save and close your Word document, and submit as directed by your instructor. **Close** any open windows.

END | You have completed Project 1D

Mastering Windows 10 | **Project 1E Create a File and Use Windows Apps**

Apply 1A skills from these Objectives:

1 Explore the Windows 10 Environment

2 Use File Explorer and Desktop Apps to Create a New Folder and Save a File

3 Identify the Functions of the Windows 10 Operating System

4 Discover Windows 10 Features

5 Sign Out of Windows 10, Turn Off Your Computer, and Manage User Accounts

6 Manage Your Windows 10 System

PROJECT ACTIVITIES

In the following Mastering Windows 10 project, you will capture and save a snip that will look similar to Figure 1.74.

 PROJECT FILES

For Project 1E, you will need the following files:

Two new Snip files that you will create during the project

You will save your files as:

Lastname_Firstname_1E_Cortana_Snip
Lastname_Firstname_1E_Snap_Snip

PROJECT RESULTS

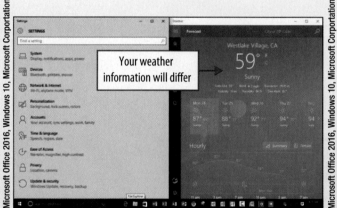

FIGURE 1.74

(Project 1E Create a File and Use Windows Apps continues on the next page)

Mastering Windows 10 | **Project 1E Create a File and Use Windows Apps** (continued)

1 Click **Start**, click **All apps**, click any letter to display an onscreen alphabet, click **G** to jump to the G section, and then click **Get Started**.

2 On the left, click **Cortana**, and then click **What is Cortana?** Scroll down to view the information about setting a reminder.

3 On the taskbar, click **Snipping Tool**, click the **New button arrow**, and then click **Window Snip**. Click anywhere in the window to capture the snip.

4 On the toolbar of the **Snipping Tool** mark-up window, click the **Highlighter**, and then highlight the text *Set a reminder*. Use the red **Pen** to circle the **hamburger menu** icon in the upper left corner. Click the **Save Snip** button.

5 In the displayed **Save As** dialog box, navigate to your **Windows 10 Chapter 1** folder. Using the jpeg file type and your own name, save the snip as **Lastname_Firstname_1E_Cortana_Snip**

6 **Close** the **Snipping Tool** window, and then **Close** the **Get Started** window.

7 Click **Start**, click **All apps**, click any letter to display an onscreen alphabet, click **S** to jump to the S section, and then click **Settings**. Display the **All apps** list again, jump to the **W** section, and then click **Weather**.

8 Press ⊞ + → to snap the Weather app to the right side of the screen. Click the **Settings** window to snap it to the left side of the screen.

9 On the taskbar, click **Snipping Tool**, click the **New button arrow**, and then click **Full-screen Snip**.

10 Click the **Save Snip** button. In the displayed **Save As** dialog box, navigate to your **Windows 10 Chapter 1** folder. Using the jpeg file type and your own name, save the snip as **Lastname_Firstname_1E_Snap_Assist_Snip**

11 Close all open windows, and then submit your two snip files to your instructor as directed.

END | You have completed Project 1E

Mastering Windows 10 **Project 1F Working with Windows, Programs, and Files**

Apply 1B skills from these Objectives:

7 Download and Extract Files and Folders

8 Use File Explorer to Display Locations, Folders, and Files

9 Start Programs and Open Data Files

10 Create, Rename, and Copy Files and Folders

11 Use OneDrive as Cloud Storage

PROJECT ACTIVITIES

In the following Mastering Windows 10 project, you will capture and save a snip that will look similar to Figure 1.75.

PROJECT FILES

For Project 1F, you will need the following files:

Two new Snip files that you will create during the project

You will save your files as:

Lastname_Firstname_1F_San_Diego_Snip
Lastname_Firstname_1F_Filter_Snip

PROJECT RESULTS

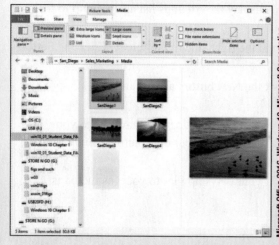

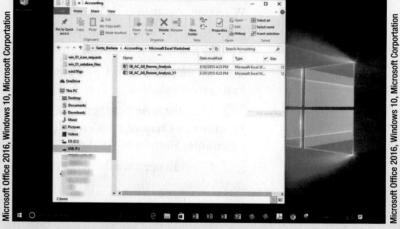

FIGURE 1.75

(Project 1F Working with Windows, Programs, and Files continues on the next page)

Mastering Windows 10 | **Project 1F Working with Windows, Programs, and Files** (continued)

1 Close all open windows, and then on the taskbar, click **File Explorer**. Display the window for your **USB flash drive**—or the location of your student data files—and then navigate to **win01_1F_Bell_Orchid ▸ San_Diego ▸ Sales_Marketing ▸ Media**.

2 From the **View tab**, change the **Layout** to **Large icons**, and then in the **file list**, click one time to select the file **SanDiego1**.

3 Display the **Preview pane** for this file.

4 Start **Snipping Tool**, create a **Window Snip**, click anywhere in the **Media** window to capture it, and then click the **Save Snip** button.

5 In the displayed **Save As** dialog box, navigate to and open your **Windows 10 Chapter 1** folder so that its name displays in the **address bar**. Using the jpeg file type and your own name, save the snip as **Lastname_Firstname_1F_San_Diego_Snip**

6 **Close** the **Snipping Tool** window. Turn off the display of the **Preview pane**. **Close** the window.

7 Open **File Explorer**, and then from your student data files, navigate to **win01_1F_Bell_Orchid ▸ Santa_Barbara ▸ Accounting**.

8 From the **Type** column heading, filter the list to display only **Microsoft Excel Worksheet** files.

9 Create a **Full-screen snip**. Using the **jpeg** file type and your own name, save the snip as **Lastname_Firstname_1F_Filter_Snip**

10 **Close** the **Snipping Tool** window. **Close** the **File Explorer** window. Submit your two snip files as directed by your instructor.

> **END | You have completed Project 1F**

OUTCOMES-BASED ASSESSMENTS

RUBRIC

The following outcomes-based assessments are *open-ended assessments*. That is, there is no specific correct result; your result will depend on your approach to the information provided. Make *Professional Quality* your goal. Use the following scoring rubric to guide you in *how* to approach the problem, and then to evaluate *how well* your approach solves the problem.

The *criteria*—Software Mastery, Content, Format and Layout, and Process—represent the knowledge and skills you have gained that you can apply to solving the problem. The *levels of performance*—Professional Quality, Approaching Professional Quality, or Needs Quality Improvements—help you and your instructor evaluate your result.

	Your completed project is of Professional Quality if you:	Your completed project is Approaching Professional Quality if you:	Your completed project Needs Quality Improvements if you:
1-Software Mastery	Choose and apply the most appropriate skills, tools, and features and identify efficient methods to solve the problem.	Choose and apply some appropriate skills, tools, and features, but not in the most efficient manner.	Choose inappropriate skills, tools, or features, or are inefficient in solving the problem.
2-Content	Construct a solution that is clear and well organized, contains content that is accurate, appropriate to the audience and purpose, and is complete. Provide a solution that contains no errors of spelling, grammar, or style.	Construct a solution in which some components are unclear, poorly organized, inconsistent, or incomplete. Misjudge the needs of the audience. Have some errors in spelling, grammar, or style, but the errors do not detract from comprehension.	Construct a solution that is unclear, incomplete, or poorly organized, contains some inaccurate or inappropriate content, and contains many errors of spelling, grammar, or style. Do not solve the problem.
3-Format and Layout	Format and arrange all elements to communicate information and ideas, clarify function, illustrate relationships, and indicate relative importance.	Apply appropriate format and layout features to some elements, but not others. Overuse features, causing minor distraction.	Apply format and layout that does not communicate information or ideas clearly. Do not use format and layout features to clarify function, illustrate relationships, or indicate relative importance. Use available features excessively, causing distraction.
4-Process	Use an organized approach that integrates planning, development, self-assessment, revision, and reflection.	Demonstrate an organized approach in some areas, but not others; or, use an insufficient process of organization throughout.	Do not use an organized approach to solve the problem.

GO! Think | Project 1G Help Desk

In this project, you will construct a solution by applying any combination of the skills you practiced from the Objectives in Projects 1A and 1B.

 PROJECT FILES

For Project 1G, you will need the following file:

win01_1G_Help_Desk (Word file)

You will save your document as:

Lastname_Firstname_1G_Help_Desk

From the student files that accompany this chapter, open the Word document **win01_1G_Help_Desk**. Save the document in your chapter folder as **Lastname_Firstname_1G_Help_Desk**

The following email question arrived at the Help Desk from an employee at the Bell Orchid Hotel's corporate office. In the Word document, construct a response based on your knowledge of Windows 10. Although an email response is not as formal as a letter, you should still use good grammar, good sentence structure, professional language, and a polite tone. Save your document and submit the response as directed by your instructor.

To: Help Desk

We have a new employee in our department, and as her user picture, she wants to use a picture of her dog. I know that Corporate Policy says it is OK to use an acceptable personal picture on a user account. Can she change the picture herself within her standard user account, or does she need an administrator account to do that?

> **END | You have completed Project 1G**

GO! Think   Project 1H Help Desk

In this project, you will construct a solution by applying any combination of the skills you practiced from the Objectives in Projects 1A and 1B.

 PROJECT FILES

For Project 1H, you will need the following file:

win01_1H_Help_Desk (Word file)

You will save your document as:

Lastname_Firstname_1H_Help_Desk

From the student files that accompany this chapter, open the Word document **win01_1H_Help_Desk**. Save the document in your chapter folder as **Lastname_Firstname_1H_Help_Desk**

The following email question arrived at the Help Desk from an employee at the Bell Orchid Hotel's corporate office. In the Word document, construct a response based on your knowledge of Windows 10. Although an email response is not as formal as a letter, you should still use good grammar, good sentence structure, professional language, and a polite tone. Save your document and submit the response as directed by your instructor.

To: Help Desk

When I'm done using my computer at the end of the day, should I use the Sleep option or the Shut down option, and what's the difference between the two?

END | You have completed Project 1H

GO Think! Project 1I Help Desk

In this project, you will construct a solution by applying any combination of the skills you practiced from the Objectives in Projects 1A and 1B.

 PROJECT FILES

For Project 1I, you will need the following file:

win01_1I_Help_Desk (Word file)

You will save your document as:

Lastname_Firstname_1I_Help_Desk

From the student files that accompany this chapter, open the Word document **win01_1I_Help_Desk**. Save the document in your chapter folder as **Lastname_Firstname_1I_Help_Desk**

The following email question has arrived at the Help Desk from an employee at the Bell Orchid Hotel's corporate office. In the Word document, construct a response based on your knowledge of Windows 10. Although an email response is not as formal as a letter, you should still use good grammar, good sentence structure, professional language, and a polite tone. Save your document and submit the response as directed by your instructor.

To: Help Desk

I am not sure about the differences between copying and moving files and folders. When is it best to copy a file or a folder and when is it best to move a file or folder? Can you also describe some techniques that I can use for copying or moving files and folders? Which do you think is the easiest way to copy or move files and folders?

END | You have completed Project 1I

Index